God's WORD Sets You Free

God's WORD Sets You Free

WITH STUDY GUIDE

Vicky Jeter

Power of One Voice, LLC

I dedicate this book to God and His Precious Love for everything He has created. I write to those searching for scriptures, learning from the only One we need, God Himself, in His Word.

May God Bless you now and forever, bringing you greater understanding each day.

God's WORD Sets You Free

Copyright © 2023 Vicky Jeter
Published by Power of OneVoice, LLC
2nd Edition
"Come Alive Series" by Vicky Jeter
All rights reserved. No portion of this book may be reproduced, stored in a retrieval system, or transmitted in any form or by any means—except for brief quotations in printed reviews, without the publisher's prior written permission.
Book design by Vicky Jeter, Power of One Voice, LLC
Unless otherwise indicated, Scripture quotations used in this book are from The New King James Version, copyright 1982 by Thomas Nelson, Inc. Used by permission. All rights reserved.
ISBN: 978-1-7378047-0-3
Printed in the United States of America

Contents

Dedication		iv
1	When the Enemy Strikes	1
2	"When The Enemy Strikes" Study	22
3	The Lie	32
4	"The Lie" Study	43
5	The Mind	61
6	"The Mind" Study	87
7	Living by Faith	98
8	"Living By Faith" Study	116
9	When Satan Goes to Church	133
10	"When Satan Goes To Church" Study	154
11	Be Strong in The Lord	176
12	"Be Strong In The Lord" Study	206
13	The Goodness of God	226
14	"The Goodness of God" Study	255

1

When the Enemy Strikes

> "Be sober, be vigilant; because your adversary the devil walks about like a roaring lion, seeking whom he may devour. Resist him, steadfast in the faith, knowing that the same sufferings are experienced by your brotherhood in the world." (1 Peter 5:8-9; NKJV)

He couldn't care less about your needs when the enemy strikes. All he thinks about is himself. Your enemy is strong, and the battles you fight are real, but today I say to you, prepare for your victory and stand up against the real enemy; Satan and his demons.

We must begin with ourselves. Put away anything that

deceives or keeps you from drawing closer to God. Be saved and begin to walk in the Word.

It will take time to weed out the things you have allowed yourself to do, first to yourself and then to others.

The storms of life are many, but there is great power in being engaged as you go thru them. God will teach new ways you need to learn and help you gain the victory you have so longed for.

Passivity and complacency are also an enemy, and God never wanted you to use these as options. He doesn't want you to fold your arms and wait for the storm to pass.

When storms come, you need to have a plan and get involved. Reading His Word is the best way to begin and sustain your walk with God. This is the way you trust God to bring you to the shore of your circumstances.

Keep in mind the best way to survive any storm is to prepare ahead of time.

Today I am very aware that I am much stronger, wiser, and more able to have victory over the enemy. This is only possible by regularly standing in the WORD of God.

The storm is not to fear but to overcome with the armor of God that has been given for us to use freely.

No seasoned fisherman or responsible ship captain sets out

across an open sea without a thorough knowledge of the vessel's equipment and without making sure all is in proper working order. They go over the navigational charts, study the weather patterns, and become acquainted with dangerous passages.

They also make sure they have supplies and equipment for every kind of circumstance they may encounter. Although no one wants to be shipwrecked, the reality is it happens.

In **1 Timothy 1:19**, we learn that being shipwrecked is often used to further warn that we can become an enemy of God's Word and the Gospel.

> "Having faith and a good conscience, which some having rejected, concerning the faith have suffered shipwreck, of whom are Hymenaeus and Alexander, whom I delivered to Satan that they may learn not to blaspheme." (1 Timothy 1:19-20; NKJV)

Keep in mind that our walk with God must continue, or else we can all experience a *shipwrecked faith*. A man who thrust away and made shipwreck of his faith, becoming a blasphemer and a false teacher, overthrowing the faith of others as we understand in **2 Timothy 2:16-18.**

> "But shun profane and idle babblings, for they will increase to more ungodliness. And their message will spread like cancer. Hymenaeus and Philetus are of this sort, who have strayed concerning the truth, saying that the resurrection is already past; and they overthrow the faith of some." (2 Timothy 2:16-18; NKJV)

God sees the heart of why we do what we do and encourages us to continue in the faith by reading and obeying His Word.

Not only in the open sea but also in life, we experience sudden trouble. This is how the enemy strikes. He suddenly turns our world upside down.

Take, for instance, Job.

Life became so difficult, so suddenly, that most of us wouldn't know how to deal with it.

It states in **Job 1:1**;

> "There was a man in the land of Uz, whose name was Job; and that man was blameless and upright, and one who feared God and shunned evil." (Job 1:1; NKJV)

Job knew God and had a daily relationship with Him, but that didn't stop storms from coming.

In **Job 1:3** it states;

> "Also, his possessions were seven thousand sheep, three thousand camels, five hundred yoke of oxen, five hundred female donkeys, and a very large household, so that this man was the greatest of all the people of the East." (Job 1:3; NKJV)

Job was always looking for ways to help others out of their misery and pray for their salvation.

In **Job 1:5,** we read that he would rise early in the morning and offer burnt offerings according to the number of his sons.

> "So it was, when the days of feasting had run their course, that Job would send and sanctify them, and he would rise early in the morning and offer burnt offerings according to the number of them all. For Job said, "It may be that my sons have sinned and cursed God in their hearts. Thus Job did regularly." (Job 1:5; NKJV)

Here in **Job,** a father simply went through religious ceremonies before God, hoping He would have mercy on his offspring.

He set them apart in his own mind and religious acts, but this did not save them or protect them even from physical death. There is no hint of their being cleansed from sin; the idea is dedicating them to God, and this is all any parent can do.

Children's actual salvation must come by meeting God's requirements for salvation.

The mention of offerings here shows that sacrifices continued from Abel's time (**Genesis 4**) through Job's time. They became an institution carried on through all the ages up to the time of Christ.

But there was more. Job was good to all people, and his heart opened wide to help them.

Let's look at **Job 29**. His past was glorious.

Here he remembers the good he did and why he did it; for God; his love for God motivated Job.

He talks about the days when God watched over him and when God's lamp shone upon his head. He talks about how by God's light, he was able to walk through darkness.

He talks about **(v 12)** that he rescued the poor who cried for help and the orphan who had no helper. But there is more.

He was eyes to the blind, feet to the lame, a father to the needy, and one who sought justice, smashed the jaws of the wicked, and snatched the prey from his teeth.

It also mentions that his glory and honor were fresh in him because he was constantly renewed.

And at the end of **chapter 29**, it says he comforted the mourners.

As you consider *who* is a Christian today, look at how they treat others less fortunate or unknowing of the Scripture on salvation.

Job didn't have the 'Blood' to save him, but he had the relationship and understanding of what it meant to walk with God in those times.

Job was a very godly man. But the attack from the enemy comes to all of us. When Satan can take your identity, he will then take your destiny. Guard yourselves lest anything worse happens to you.

Although Job was prepared in many ways by the life he lived, he went through the worst times, losing everything, including his health. He had nothing left but God and his faith in God. But he also asked God many times, 'Why'?

Here's some of the story. It began like this, as we read in **Job 1:6;**

> "Now there was a day when the sons of God came to present themselves before the LORD, and Satan also came among them." (Job 1:6; NKJV)

This is the first mention, historically speaking, of the arch-enemy of God and man, by name. Not even in Genesis is he mentioned by name, and the time of Job was early in history, for he was the son of Issachar, the son of Jacob **(Genesis 46:13).**

It is clear in **Genesis 3** that there was an invisible enemy who caused the fall of man, but in the passage, he is shown using the serpent as a tool in the same way that he used Peter in **Matthew 16:23**.

> "But He turned and said to Peter, "Get behind Me, Satan! You are an offense to Me, for you are not mindful of the things of God, but the things of men."
> (Matthew 16:23; NKJV)

In **Job 41,** he is symbolized by a great dragon. He is the evil spirit working in the children of disobedience throughout the ages **(Ephesians 2:1-3).**

Here he is named and spoken of as a real person with access to heaven and power to accuse the brethren and seek their destruction **(Revelations 12:9-12).**

The word "Satan" means adversary and accuser. Don't take lightly what Satan can and does accomplish, driving a wedge between all of us. He is the archenemy of good; and works through us *if we allow him.*

Job 1:7-12 is where the LORD had a conversation with Satan. He shared that Job was a blameless and upright man who feared Him with reverence and honored God, turning away from evil.

Satan challenged the LORD. Satan said to God that He had given him so much and that he is happy because of all this, but if you take away all he has, he will curse you to your face.

Satan wanted to prove Job's obedience and service were only because of the good things he received.

And so, the LORD allowed Satan to challenge Job.

These challenges are meant to build our faith in God and *not tempt us to sin.* God doesn't tempt us, causing us to sin.

God only wants us to grow stronger in Him.

In a quick and harsh sweep of back-to-back calamities, Job is broken and in grief.

The extraordinary accumulation of the disasters he dealt with would have been devastating to any of us.

Job is now left bankrupt, homeless, helpless, and childless. He's left weeping over the ten fresh graves of his now-dead children. His wife is overcome with grief as she kneels beside him.

Then Job says in **Job 1:20-22**;

> "Then Job arose, tore his robe, and shaved his head; and he fell to the ground and worshipped. And he said: "Naked I came from my mother's womb, and naked shall I return there. The LORD gave, and the LORD has taken away; Blessed be the name of the LORD." In all this Job did not sin nor charge God with wrong." (Job 1:20-22; NKJV)

In **v 19, a cyclone or hurricane** struck the house where Job's sons and daughters were feasting.

When Job received the report **(v 20)** of the destruction of his sons and daughters, his eldest son's house, his livestock (valued at around $790,000), and no doubt his crops where the oxen were plowing **(v 14)**, he simply arose and refused to blame God as Satan had hoped he would **(v 11, 20-22)**.

But Job in **(v 21)** praised God for the works of the devil; by believing that God took everything away and not understanding that God doesn't do that.

There were two great mistakes of Job. The first one is in claiming the Lord has taken away **(v 21)**. We must understand that the Lord didn't take away but *Satan did this* **(Job 1:6-19)**.

The second one is in *questioning*; shall we not accept adversity **(Job 2:10)**? God cannot tempt men with evil. **(James 1:13-16)**.

> "Let no one say when he is tempted, "I am tempted by God"; for God cannot be tempted by evil, nor does He Himself tempt anyone. But each one is tempted when he is drawn away by his own desires and enticed. Then, when desire has conceived, it gives birth to sin; and sin, when it is full-grown, brings forth death. Do not be deceived, my beloved brethren." (James 1:13-16; NKJV)

We are to pray "deliver us from evil"—not "deliver us from God" **(Matthew 6:13).**

Job was like many others *who think* that sickness, disease, calamity, and other evils come from God and that Satan has nothing to do with them.

Christians indeed experience tests of faith, persecutions, injustices, and trials of life, but *they are not required* to suffer sickness, disease, or poverty *in order to be saved and in the will of God.*

The tests Joseph went through in Egypt **(Genesis 39-41)**, Stephen suffered from the Jews **(Acts 7),** and Paul experienced— beatings, buffetings, dangers, perils, slander, lies, distress, hunger, nakedness, stonings, imprisonments, shipwrecks, and other things of **2 Corinthians 11**—were not the same kind as sickness, disease, and the curses of sin and rebellion which Christ died to free us from.

Nevertheless, these were also caused by Satan and evil men, not *God*. God was not responsible for the things which caused Joseph, Stephen, and Paul to suffer. God helped them through the things Satan and his agents heaped upon them.

God can teach us lessons from any kind of trial, but He does not necessarily send trials in order to teach us such lessons.

A father could use the experience of his son, should he break the law and suffer penalties in jail, as an occasion to teach certain lessons for the betterment of the son's future, but it would be a very ungodly father who would lead him into such troubles for the particular purpose of teaching those lessons which could be taught otherwise.

Thus, it is with us. We do not need to experience sickness, disease, poverty, and accidents in order to learn what we should know from God.

We have been given examples in the Word: Job, Asa, Hezekiah, and many more.

We can best glorify God by learning through these examples and becoming an example ourselves, one experiencing God's blessing by being kept from such troubles and sufferings.

Enough sinners and unbelievers are giving us examples without Christians going through needless suffering.

It is not the will of God for us to suffer.

In the Word of God, provision has been made through the "exceedingly great and precious promises" to give us "all things that pertain to life and godliness" **(2 Corinthians 1:20; 2 Peter 1:3-4).**

> **"For all the promises of God in Him are Yes, and in Him Amen, to the glory of God through us." (2 Corinthians 1:20; NKJV)**

All God's promises are "Yes and so be it" or "Yes and truth." In Him, they are always yes, and in Him, they are always truthful.

Not one promise of God is "no" to the one who will believe and meet the conditions.

To prepare for the enemy, we need to know the ONE who cares. Fear of the unknown is what Satan uses to cripple us. Unless you know scripture and read it regularly, you will be fearful.

But God is faithful and never left us without the ability to stand against the enemy.

Satan wanted to hurt Job even more.

And then Satan tells the Lord that if you take away his health, he will curse You to Your face. The Lord allows Satan's hand upon Job but tells him to not kill him.

Then his wife tells Job to curse God and die. This is how the enemy strikes. This challenge was for us to read and understand thru the ages.

We experience similar circumstances when we don't know God and those around us say things such as Job's wife. We suffer because of our lack of understanding, not because God is causing us to suffer.

When we raise our children, it is the same. They suffer because of their lack of understanding of how we are trying to protect them.

We remain stuck in this state of mind because we don't know God; but have only heard about Him through others, other religions, etc.

It was a sobering thought to put things into perspective in how Job perceived everything and what he had to experience about all these trials.

We see his story and how it all turned out, but he didn't see it that way.

It's true for us also, as we go through trials. We don't have any assurance of how it will all turn out. We are asked to trust God and have the faith to know that He is always looking out for our good and doesn't want us to suffer.

Satan wants us to suffer and destroy all our good efforts and intents by bringing evil upon us and those we love.

Satan is a dirty rat fink who has done this to everyone. We

can learn how to keep Satan away from our lives when we see him as he is.

Job never knew how it would end as he walked thru it. As he continued to suffer daily severe loss of earthly things, family, and his health, Job had only one sure thing left to cling to: God.

When the inspired writer used Job as an example, it was not to picture him as a weak, helpless, powerless, unbelieving, rebellious person, ignorant about appropriating the benefits of the gospel.

It was to encourage Christians to believe in God for the healing promised in **James 5:14-18.**

In the end, God healed and blessed Job materially beyond anything he had experienced before his trial, and so it is the plan of God for all, not just Job.

It is clear from Scripture that Job's trouble was of Satan and not of God (**Job 1:6-19; 2:1-7**).

The LORD was the deliverer of Job (**Job 42:1-10**).

Christ came to heal all who were oppressed by the devil, not oppressed by God (**Matthew 8:17; Luke 13:16; John 10:10; Acts 10:38; 1 Peter 2:24**).

To follow the truth, we should stop blaming God for sickness, pain, poverty, and calamity and count them as curses or enemies of God and man.

And then cooperate with God and look to Him for deliverance and immunity from these thoughts and beliefs.

After listening to God speak in four chapters, Job confessed that he had *reasoned wrongly* while trying to figure out why everything was happening to him.

He says in **Job 42:2 & 3**;

> "I know that You can do everything, And that no purpose of Yours can be withheld from You. You asked, 'Who is this who hides counsel without knowledge?' Therefore, I have uttered what I did not understand, Things too wonderful for me, which I did not know."
> (Job 42:2-3; NKJV)

And then, in **v 4,** Job was completely done with his complaints of injustice. He knew that his presuppositions were wrong and needed God's wisdom.

Much of the book of Job is a story of trying to figure out why God is doing this to him. His friends and Job himself converse. But God listens and lets each talk.

The same happens today. God allows us to work thru things, and ultimately God hopes we will return to a greater understanding, the one we find in His Word.

The trials of life are meant for us to grow in understanding. Job was not convicted of a particular sin but of too small a view of God.

However, Job also learned that although difficult at times, one must simply trust God without knowing everything about why things happened.

We must use these times to pray and spend quality time in the WORD. God will heal you from within.

It is my experience; having walked through some very lonely and misunderstood times, I have finally realized how important these times were in building my relationship with God and trusting Him through it all.

In the past, I might have become more dependent on others to fix things, spiritually and earthly; but instead, I spent a lot of time reading God's Word from cover to cover, and this was when God began to miraculously change everything in my thinking and in my daily life.

The Bible reveals God's character and person and becomes

the very tool through which *we begin to evaluate our own selves*. I found this to be the power that changed me.

Upon my commitment to read daily the Bible, I began to shed the scales that were heavy on my being. I began a transformation, and to this day, I cannot explain how it happens.

<u>It only happened by reading the Word daily, and God did it all.</u> ***It was a miracle!***

Isaiah shares his own vision of God in **Isaiah 6**. Here we see the glory of God, and although it transcends the universe, Isaiah emphasizes God's closeness to His creation and involvement with the earth and all people.

Job realized the same as Isaiah did, that our greatest failing is realizing who God is and His character.

Most of our lives, we are so caught up in the mundane that we don't understand and experience God's holiness as we should. There is little appreciation or understanding of the sacred part of God.

We have too often reduced Him to only friend and advisor. Maybe Job began to see that God was more than he had thought.

The experience of coming to understand God in a whole new way was humbling, challenging, and exhilarating.

Job regretted that his trust in God had been so imperfect, for he now understood God in a deeper way.

The beauty is that in the end, Job had *a new relationship* with the Lord.

After everything he went through, I believe that Job's life became so rich in the fruits of the spirit. His faith and trust grew exceedingly, and he understood how much God was his friend. Job also must have understood how to watch out for what the enemy is always waiting to do to him or anyone else.

I would have loved to hear more about Job in his latter days, but that is left for eternity when we can visit with him personally.

It says in **Job 42:5;**

> **"I have heard of You by the hearing of the ear, but now my eye sees You." (Job 42:5; NKJV)**

The story of Job is also God reminding us that we must be ready when the enemy strikes.

Satan is real, and we will experience him all throughout our lives. However, each time we can grow in trust and in faith in our relationship with God.

We endure trials that we don't deserve, but they are permitted. Just like in the story of Job.

We also learn that thru these experiences, there is a mystery of God's unfathomable Will.

These elements sometimes are things we can never fully understand or explain, but one day we will see how these things changed us like nothing ever could.

Don't try to figure everything out; tell God you trust Him. Don't let things make you increasingly more confused. They will eventually cause resentment and bitterness in your heart.

Job never really knew "why" about so much, but when he went home, he did understand even more.

Remember that we have an enemy, and he will strike us, but we have an even more powerful, unseen Defender, God.

Although our questions are often unanswered, and the silence of God's voice makes us wonder if He is even here, He is here, and He does care, and that is what you build your trust in.

God is speaking to you today, but you must go to where God is. Holy Spirit is there to teach you everything; as you study the WORD.

2

"When The Enemy Strikes" Study

FURTHER STUDY

7 Commands for Christians
(1 Peter 1:13-22; NKJV)

1. Gird up the loins of your mind.

This means to brace up and take courage in face of the trials that one is called to go through.
What does this verse say about "rest"?

_____

2. Be sober.

The Greek word used is *nepho*, which means to live soberly and righteously. Also, see **Titus 2:11-12 and 1 Thessalonians 5:6-8**. *Nepho* refers to not drinking intoxicants but living soberly, righteously, and watching. Even among the heathen, drunk during the day was considered a disgrace. Paul encouraged them to live as children of the light and the day.

What was Paul telling the Christians to put on, and why was this important (1 Thessalonians 5:6-8)?

_____
_____
_____
_____

3. Rest your hope fully upon the grace and salvation that are to be brought at the coming of Christ (1 Peter 1:13; Romans 8:24-25).

In Romans 8:24-25 what are we saved in? How are we to wait for what we do not see? And why?

_____
_____

_____
_____
_____

(Philippians 3:21; 1 Corinthians 15:51-58)

4. Do not live according to your former life of sin (1 Peter 1:14; Ephesians 2:1-3).

You are new creatures, and you must live new lives.
Read 2 Corinthians 5:17-18.
Salvation is changing how you do things outwardly and inwardly.
When we are in Christ, what do these verses say we become? How is our life changed? Now all things are of what?

_____
_____
_____
_____

In 1 Peter 1:14, what are we not to conform to?

_____
_____

5. Be holy in all your manner of life (1 Peter 1:15).

You are to imitate God in all things **(1 Peter 1:16).**
Here we see Peter talking about the importance of how we

live. Peter explains that Christianity has an infinite advantage over paganism. God is holy and calls for all His followers to be like Him.

Why is this so important? Do you see a need to change from how you lived as a worldly follower?

_____
_____
_____
_____

Hebrew 12:14 tells why change is important for us and how we can and should be an example to a lost world. Explain why it's important.

_____
_____
_____
_____

6. Pass the time of your stay here, as a believer, in fear.

Fear isn't to cause you deep emotional distress but to warn you that the enemy is still at large, and you need to stay close to the Father who now protects you.

In **1 Corinthians 10:12-13** Paul beautifully gives assurance of the eternal keeping of God in all temptations and His help in every one of them, providing we are in obedience, watching for the warnings.

No man can be kept from a fall if he persistently refuses to meet the conditions.

In 1 Corinthians 10:12-13 what is the first warning Paul writes about (1 Peter 1:12)? How does God help you when you are tempted (1 Peter 1:13)?

_____
_____
_____
_____
_____

7. See that you love one another fervently with a pure heart. (1 Peter 1:22; John 13:34-35; John 15:12-13).

7 New Natures of Born-Again Believers
1 Peter 1:22-23

1. _____
2. _____
3. _____
4. _____
5. _____
6. _____
7. _____

In John 13:34-35 we read of a New Commandment.

"A new commandment I give to you, that you love one another, as I have loved you, that you also love one another. By this all will know that you are My disciples if you have love for one another." ***(John 13:34-35; NKJV)***

This is the same as the old commandment in **Leviticus 19:18**, *".... but you shall love your neighbor as yourself...."* ***(Leviticus 19:18; NKJV)***

The renewed commandment here has an additional part, "as I have loved you."

Christ more than fulfilled the Mosaic precept, He not only loved His neighbor as Himself, but He loved him more than Himself, for He laid down His own life for others.

In **John 13:35,** Christ virtually said to them, 'You have been ambitious, envious, and at strife for supremacy. This cannot be. You must love as I love. By this shall all men know you to be Christians.'

Disciples of different teachers were known by their habits or some particular creed or rite, but the disciples of Christ were to be known by the love they had for one another.

Loving because it's easy isn't what this is talking about.

Christ died for all and not just those who turn to Him.

He died for all. To love others when they don't seem to agree with you is God's way of loving all.

This is how you can know if someone is truly walking with Christ. If they don't love, then love is not in them.

We are all a work in progress and can make changes to be more Christ-like.

If we are known by habits of living our lives, what things can you change in your own life to become more like Christ?

_____

_____

_____

God's Purpose in Allowing Satan to Continue

To develop character and faith in the believer. (**James 1:12; 1 Peter 1:7-13; 5:8-9; 2 Peter 1:4-9; Jude 20-24**).

In **1 Peter 1:7** (NKJV), what kind of faith is written about that God wants to create in you?

_____

God's WORD Sets You Free

To keep the believer humble. **(2 Corinthians 12:7-9).**

Paul describes the thorn in the flesh as a messenger of Satan. He accepted this as a help to keep him on track for the Lord. In vs. 9, what two things did God give Paul because of his willingness to accept that God knew what was best for him?

_____

To provide a conflict for saints that they may be rewarded through overcoming. **(1 John 2:13; 4:1-6; Revelations 2:7, 11, 17, 26-28; 3:5, 12, 21).**

Who was the "conflict" John was referring to in **1 John 2:13**? (NKJV)

_____

To demonstrate the power of God over the power of Satan. **(Mark 16:17-20; 1 Corinthians 4:9; Ephesians 2:7; 3:10).**

In **Mark 16:17** (NKJV), what signs will follow the believers, and what will they be able to cast out?

_____

To use him in afflicting people to bring them to repentance. **(1 Corinthians 5:1-6; 2 Corinthians 2:5-11; Job 33:14-30).**

Why would it be encouraged to bring people to the seriousness of their sin (**1 Corinthians 5:1-5, NKJV**)? Is God being mean or merciful? What is God's ultimate desire for His children?

_____
_____
_____

To purge man of all possibility of failing in the eternal future. **(Revelations 21).**

Does our future home look like something you are willing to change your ways to have for all eternity as we read **Revelations 21?** Is it worth living right to have one day a life forever with God and all He wants to give you? If the earth has many things as Heaven does, can you imagine the amazing place Planet Heaven is? What are your thoughts?

_____
_____
_____
_____

Power of One Voice, LLC
Come Alive Series

3

The Lie

> "But I fear, lest somehow, as the serpent deceived Eve by his craftiness, so your minds may be corrupted from the simplicity that is in Christ." (2 Corinthians 11:3; NKJV)

It all became clear in the beginning. Genesis is all about the beginnings, and the first lie told to Eve presents to us why we struggle.

In **Genesis 3:4,** we see the first lie. It was a direct lie:

> "Then the serpent said to the woman "You will not surely die." (Genesis 3:4; NKJV)

Satan used the weapon of his choice and is still using it today. He lies to us and gets us to not look at the truth.

The truth will set you free, but are you looking for it? And where are you looking to find it?

There is only one authority when questioning religion: the Word of God. So, if you need to know something is right, simply look for answers in the Word of God.

With no introduction, Satan appears in the Garden of Eden. Interestingly, Eve expressed no surprise at the serpent speaking to her intelligibly.

In **Revelations 12,** we read about the age-old serpent, the devil, called Satan, who continually deceives and secures the entire inhabited world.

Jesus talks with the Jewish who claim to be the children of God; he explains that they are children of Satan in **John 8:44;**

> "You are of your father the devil, and the desires of your father you want to do. He was a murderer from the beginning, and does not stand in the truth, because there is no truth in him. When he speaks a lie, he speaks from his own resources, for he is a liar and the father of it." (John 8:44; NKJV)

In this verse, the Greek word used for "devil" is *diabolos*, adversary, slanderer, the accuser. It is used of Satan here and in **John 13:2**;

> "And supper being ended, the devil having already put it into the heart of Judas Iscariot, Simon's son, to betray Him." (John 13:2; NKJV)

But the first lie Satan told was to Eve, and she begins to believe his lie.

Satan casts doubt. He didn't deny that God had spoken but put doubt in Eve's mind. He simply made Eve question whether God had said what Eve *thought* He had said.

Perhaps Eve just misunderstood, was Satan's suggestion. It was subtle and not attacking in the way he said it. Satan planted thoughts that Eve owes it to herself to rethink what He said.

However, Satan was also questioning, in a subtle way, God's goodness. He was suggesting that if God was good, He wouldn't keep something from you.

Satan did the same thing to Jesus in the wilderness. He said that if you are God's beloved Son, why are you hungry?

God's WORD Sets You Free

Mocking God's Word. It was a short step from questioning God's Word to denying it. Because Adam and Eve had never experienced "death," they could only trust God's Word.

But when the serpent came and cast doubt *in their minds*, they stopped trusting God and started listening to the voice of the serpent.

In Adam and Eve's unique situation where they were the first; and only had God to trust, God also made sure that His Word was all they *needed*.

In **Genesis 3:4,** the serpent says to Eve that she will certainly not die!

The serpent is your enemy Satan, and he is always full of double motives and cunning in his purpose.

Satan was trying to gain favor and trust with Eve, and that is what happened. However, Eve may have already been questioning things, and it was easier for her to trust in someone other than God.

We read in **2 Corinthians 11:3-4** a warning to us all in any situation where we deviate from following God and His Word!

> "But I fear, lest somehow, as the serpent deceived Eve by his craftiness, so your minds may be corrupted from the simplicity that is in Christ. For if he who comes preaches another Jesus whom we have not preached, or if you receive a different spirit which you have not received, or a different gospel which you have not accepted—you may well put up with it!" (2 Corinthians 11:3-4; NKJV)

Here Paul fears for his own converts that they may be turned away from Christ, as Eve was deceived by Satan to turn away from God.

In **verse 4,** Paul refers to the false apostle who had come to Corinth after he had left.

Satan defends his lie. It is revealed in **Isaiah 14:13-14** that Satan said in his heart that he would ascend to heaven, raising his own throne above the stars of God and that he would sit on the mount of assembly....and finally, he says that he will make himself like the Most High.

> "For you have said in your heart: 'I will ascend into heaven, I will exalt my throne above the stars of God; I will also sit on the mount of the congregation on the farthest sides of the north; I will ascend above the

> **heights of the clouds, I will be like the Most High.'"**
> **(Isaiah 14:13-14; NKJV)**

Although Adam and Eve knew they were already made in the image of God, Satan persisted in tempting them with an even greater privilege: to be like God. This was Satan's greatest ambition when he was Lucifer, God's angelic servant.

Keep in mind that Satan is a created being by God, who oversaw worshipping God, but he wanted to be worshipped and served like the Creator.

This attitude led him to rebel against God and seek to establish his own kingdom.

"You will be like God" is the biggest lie that has controlled mankind since the fall.

In Romans, we read that they exchanged the truth of God for a lie and worshipped and served the creature rather than the Creator.

This lie controls so many things in our world today. Man is seeking to pull himself up and build his own utopia, by his own strength.

Eve's sin began when she started to question or forget the grace of God and the goodness of God.

In **Genesis 3:2**, Eve *omitted* the word *"freely."*

> "And the woman said to the serpent, "We may eat the fruit of the trees of the garden;" (Genesis 3:2; NKJV)

God's original word in **Genesis 2:16** clearly states;

> "And the LORD God commanded the man, saying, "Of every tree of the garden you may freely eat;" (Genesis 2:16; NKJV)

Maybe Satan had planted the thought in Eve's mind that God was holding out on her.

Eve then added to God's Word. She says in **Genesis 3:3** that God said she couldn't touch the fruit.

> "But of the fruit of the tree which is in the midst of the garden, God has said, 'You shall not eat it, nor shall you touch it, lest you die.'" (Genesis 3:3; NKJV)

The woman misquoted the words from God, implying doubt as to whether the penalty would be executed; as we read in **Genesis 2:17;**

> **"But of the tree of the knowledge of good and evil you shall not eat, for in the day that you eat of it you shall surely die." (Genesis 2:17; NKJV)**

It is written in **1 John 5:3** that, "His commandments are not burdensome".

Satan wants us to believe they are a burden and that Satan can offer us something better.

As Satan presented it, the penalty for disobedience did not seem as harsh. So, Eve considered forsaking God's Will and obeying Satan's will.

This lie opened the human mind's door to listen to Satan.

Once we treat God's Word in this fashion, we become wide open to the devil's final trick.

Satan simply caused Eve to consider the tree *apart* from God's

Word. He got into her mind and planted thoughts, reasonings, and doubts.

God accomplishes His Will on earth through "truth" found in the Word of God, but Satan accomplishes it through "lies."

When we believe in God's Truth, the Spirit of God can work in power, as stated in **John 16:13**.

> **"However, when He, the Spirit of truth, has come, He will guide you into all truth; for He will not speak on His own authority, but whatever He hears He will speak; and He will tell you things to come. (John 16:13; NKJV)**

But when we believe a lie, Satan goes to work in that lie, as stated in **John 8:44**.

> **"You are of your father the devil, and the desires of your father you want to do. He was a murderer from the beginning, and does not stand in the truth, because there is no truth in him. When he speaks a lie, he speaks from his own resources, for he is a liar and the father of it." (John 8:44; NKJV)**

Faith in God's truth leads to victory, but faith in Satan's lies leads to defeat. However, Satan doesn't advertise that "this is a lie" because he's good at masquerading his lies as God's Truth.

As we read in **2 Corinthians 11:13-14;**

> **"For such are false apostles, deceitful workers, transforming themselves into apostles of Christ. And no wonder! For Satan himself transforms himself into an angel of light."** (2 Corinthians 11:13-14; NKJV)

Satan disguises himself as an angel of light. And when he approached Eve, he didn't come in his true nature; he put on a mask to disguise himself. He probably was kind and gentle but suggestive, and Eve felt safe around him.

Throughout scripture, we read of counterfeit Christians, counterfeit gospels, counterfeit ministers of the gospel, counterfeit righteousness, counterfeit "churches," counterfeit doctrines, and counterfeit Christ—the Antichrist, who will accept for Satan the worship and service of the whole world.

Bottom line it is a battlefield in the mind. Satan's target is your mind, and his weapon is his lies and his dominion currently on earth.

My personal success has only come from staying focused on being a student of God's Word. It has grounded me because I listen to God and remember what He says.

The Word of God, The Bible, is truly your defense against the enemy. Learn it, remember it, and apply it to your life.

If you are like me, having left a church you once trusted, don't fret. God has something better. While you are looking, start daily reading at least 30 minutes of "quiet reading" in the Word and work up to a longer time when possible. This will give you a greater advantage to re-direct your walk and help you grow.

God will teach you, walk with you, and share things you need to know. God is your comfort, teacher, and best friend....so don't go out into the world without Him beside you.

Religion will never save you, but God's Word will. The Bible is your go-to source for everything.

4

"The Lie" Study

FURTHER STUDY

9 Facts About Lucifer
(Isaiah 14:12)

He was cast out of heaven **(v 12; Luke 10:18)**. If he fell from heaven, he must have been cast out; he must have ascended to heaven in the first place to be cast out. There was some reason for him going there and not staying there after he got there. It must have been a forced and bodily casting out, a departure because of superior power and forces. What kind of fall does **Luke 10:18** describe?

_____

He was forcibly intercepted in his invasion of heaven and was defeated and cast down. He found himself back on the earth he ascended from, which he ruled before his fall and invasion of heaven. **Ezekiel 28:17** gives the cause of Satan's fall. What caused it?

_____

He had already weakened the nations (**v 12; Ezekiel 28:11-17**). This means that before his invasion of heaven, he had weakened the nations of earth over whom he had ruled since the creation of the earth and its inhabitants. Is he still up to no good?

_____

In **v 13**, Lucifer says, "I will ascend into heaven." This is one of the things Lucifer said in his heart when planning to overthrow God in heaven. According to **Colossians 1:15-18**, God created thrones, dominion, principalities, and powers, visible and invisible, in heaven and on earth. Lucifer was given dominion of the earth and worked deceitfully to get other angelic rulers to follow him in his war against God. How many angels fell with him, as said in **Revelations 12:1-12**?

_____

In **Isaiah 14:13**, Lucifer says, "I will exalt my throne above the stars of God." This proves that Lucifer's plan was to invade heaven, dethrone God, and become the supreme ruler of all creations, and it shows that he already was a ruler. If he had a throne, he had a kingdom and was a king. He had subjects to rule, and there must have been a location for the kingdom.

"I will also sit on the mount of the congregation on the farthest sides of the north" **(v 13)**.

Lucifer was not satisfied with sitting on his own throne but also wanted to sit on God's throne to be worshiped as the Supreme Sovereign of all creations. Heaven is a planet, as the Word says.

Psalm 75:6-7 gives the location or direction of heaven. What does it say?

_____

"I will ascend above the heights of the clouds" (v 14). In **Matthew 25:41**, what does it say that hell was prepared for?

_____

"I will be like the Most High" **(v 14)**. This was Lucifer's reason to cause all the sinful and rebellious activities. It is noble to desire to be like God or imitate Him in His consecration to the highest good of all. But to transgress the laws of God and become selfish and devoted to a life of self-gratification at the expense of all is the greatest of all crimes among free moral agents. Lucifer wanted to become like God at the expense of God and all who opposed him; this was extreme sinfulness against God and nature. It was by this appeal to be like God that Eve was deceived, as we read in **Genesis 3:4-5.** What did Satan tell Eve that she could have and reflected the whole reason for his rebellion?

___

"You shall be brought down to Sheol." **(v 15)**. This will be the final doom of Satan and all who follow him. **(Matthew 25:21; Revelations 20:10)**. Who is already there according to **Revelations 20:10**?

___

7 Steps in Temptation
(James 1:14-15)

1. Tempted—an evil thought **(v 14)**.

2. Drawn away—strong imagination **(v 14)**.

3. Desires—delight in viewing it **(v 14)**.

4. Enticed—weakening of the will **(v 14)**.

5. Desire conceived—yielding **(v 15)**.

6. Sin—a sinful act committed **(v 15)**.

7. Death—the result of actual sin **(v 15)**.

<u>7 Commands to Christians</u>
(James 1:19-22)

1. Be swift to hear **(v 19)**.

2. Be slow to speak **(v 19)**.

3. Be slow to wrath **(v 19)**.

4. Lay aside all filthiness **(v 21)**.

5. Lay aside all overflowing of wickedness **(v 21)**.

6. Receive the Word with meekness **(v 21)**.

7. Be doers of the Word **(v 22)**.

There are no unconditional promises or covenants in Scripture. God needs each to choose to live better or right even after a life of sin.

God's love is always looking for a way to save each of us, even if that is in our final breath.

10 Commands for Backsliders
(James 4:7-11)

1. Submit yourselves to God **(v 7)**.

2. Resist the devil **(v 7)**.

3. Draw near to God **(v 8)**.

4. Cleanse your hands, you sinners **(v 8)**.

5. Purify your hearts, you doubters **(v 8)**.

6. Lament and mourn and weep **(v 9)**.

7. Let your laughter be turned to mourning **(v 9)**.

8. Let your joy be turned to gloom **(v 9)**.

9. Humble yourself before God **(v 10)**.

10. Do not speak evil of one another **(v 11)**.

God's 4 Promises to Backsliders
(James 4:7)

1. God gives more grace to the humble.

2. He (the devil) will flee from you.

God's WORD Sets You Free

3. He (God) will draw near to you.

4. He (God) shall lift you up.

1 Peter 5:9

What method of satanic defeat is open to every child of God? **(see also James 4:7)**

_____
_____
_____
_____

What 7 Christian virtues guarantee security in Christ?
(2 Peter 1:4-9)

1. _____

2. _____

3. _____

4. _____

5. _____

6. _____

7. _____

7 Final Commands to Christians (Jude 20-23)

1. Build yourselves up on your most holy faith **(v 20; 1 Timothy 1:4)**.

2. Pray in the Holy Spirit **(v 20, Ephesians 6:18; Romans 8:26)**.

3. Keep yourselves in the love of God **(v 21; 2 Timothy 1:14; Romans 8:35-39)**.

4. Look for the mercy of our Lord Jesus Christ **(v 21; Hebrews 12:15)**.

5. Have compassion on some, making a distinction between those who are weak and ignorant and those who are proud and arrogant of heart and unwilling to obey the truth **(v 22)**.

6. Save the willing with fear, pulling them out of the fate of eternal hell **(v 23)**.

God's WORD Sets You Free

7. Hate even the garment defiled by the flesh (**v 23; James 1:27; Ephesians 5:27**).

Paul's Thorn in The Flesh
(2 Corinthians 12:7-10)

Some have said this thorn is a disease or infirmity, but this is not what Paul is talking about. In **2 Corinthians 12:7**, it tells what that thorn was.

What is it, or who is it?

_____

Paul's thorn is best understood when reading **Numbers 33:55; Ezekiel 28:24;** and **Hosea 2:6,** where the same Greek word, *skolops,* is used as a thorn, is found in the Septuagint (the Greek version of the Old Testament).

In **Numbers 33:55,** we read that when you allow wrong things in your life...

> "But if you do not drive out the _____ of the land from before you, then it shall be that those whom you let _____ shall be _____ in your eyes and thorns in _____, and they

> shall _____ you in the land where you
> _____." (NKJV)

In **Ezekiel 28:24**, we read:

> "And there shall no longer be a
> _____ or a _____ for
> the house of Israel from among all who are around
> them, who despise them. Then they shall know that I
> am the Lord GOD." (NKJV)

In **Hosea 2:6**, we read:

> "Therefore, behold, I will _____ up
> your way with thorns, and _____ her
> in, so that she cannot find her paths." (NKJV).

The prediction is that she would not be happy and successful in her life of harlotry and would long for her husband again and return to him (**v 9-10**).

God's WORD Sets You Free

The simplest explanation of the thorn in the flesh that God or man can give in **2 Corinthians 12:7** reveals it as a *messenger of Satan*. The Greek word used for messenger is *angelos* which means angel and is translated 179 times as angel. It is never translated as disease or physical infirmity and never means any such thing. An angel of Satan, one of the spirit beings which fell with him, followed Paul and buffeted him when he was tempted to become exalted. Paul lists some of the things this angel caused him to go through to keep him humble in **2 Corinthians 11:23-27**. There is not a disease in the whole list.

In **2 Corinthians 12:8-9** God assures Paul that this angel of Satan was in His will, that grace would be provided to suffer all things, and that Paul should learn to depend wholly upon the power of God.

Thorns provide a conflict for saints that they may be rewarded through overcoming (**1 John 2:13: 1 John 4:1-6; Revelations 2:7, 11, 26-28; Revelations 3:5, 12, 21**).

What is the conflict for saints in **1 John 2:13**?

_____

What is the conflict for saints in **1 John 4:1-3**?

_____

What is the blessing for saints in **Revelations 2:7?**

_____

What is the blessing for saints in **Revelations 3:12?**

_____

Thorns can demonstrate the power of God over the power of Satan **(Mark 16:17-18; Ephesians 2:7; Ephesians 3:10)**

What power from God is given to the saints in **Mark 16:17-18?**

_____

_____

What will God show in the ages to come **(Ephesians 2:7)?**

God's WORD Sets You Free

_____

_____

What will be made known by the church **(Ephesians 3:10)**?

_____

_____

5. Thorns can be used in afflicting people to bring them to repentance **(1 Corinthians 5:1-6; 2 Corinthians 2:5-11; Job 33:14-30)**

What type of sin was Paul talking about in **1 Corinthians 5:1-6**?

_____

_____

Why did Paul ask them to separate from those who felt no remorse or wrongdoing in this sin?

_____

_____

After they were allowed to be given over to the desires of the flesh, what result was God hoping for? **(v 5)**

_____

_____

In **Job 33:14-30** God reveals His will and purpose, and when a man is brought low and turns to God, a mediator from God is sent with His message **(v 23)**. If the chastened one accepts God, he is both saved and healed. **(v 24-28)**. The reason for God's dealings is found in **v 29-30**.

> "Behold, God works all these things, twice, in fact, three times with a man, To bring back _____ from the Pit, that he may be _____ with the _____ of life. (Job 33:29-30; NKJV)

<u>Forgers of Lies</u>
(Job 13:4)

> "But you forgers of lies, you are all worthless physicians." (Job 13:4)

The lies here were perhaps false accusations, errors, and false positions.

These friends did not see the truth of the divine dealings, Job's character, or Satan's works.

They maintained that Job was a hypocrite, that God was punishing him for his sins, and that the Almighty dealt with men according to their character in this world, all of which Job regarded as false doctrine.

They had come to console him and to sympathize with him, but nothing they had said helped him in the least. He only became more provoked to utter things he did not want.

These friends were worthless doctors to him.

Have you ever experienced these kinds of friends? I have so often, yet the only way to not let the deception, running rampant 'in their minds,' affect you is to walk away.

Job's Plea to His Friends *(Job 13:6)*

> "Now hear my reasoning, and heed the pleadings of my lips." (Job 13:6)

Job is asking for his friends to give him a hearing so he can plead his own case.

Keep reading **(v 6-13)**.

He says; will you speak deceitfully and wickedly and then claim that you are speaking for God? Will you be partial to God and show injustice for my cause? Will you be special pleaders in His stead? Will it be well with you when He puts you on trial? Don't your arguments mock God? He will surely reprove you if you show partiality. You should treat me as justly as you would God. Can you deceive Him like a man? Shouldn't you be afraid of Him? Your weighty sayings are like ashes; your arguments crumble like lumps of clay. Be silent, let me alone that I may speak, and then let come what will **(v 6-13)**.

As we read this plea from Job, who is unjustly condemned by those who have probably called themselves 'friends' for quite a while, does it remind you of situations you have gone through? It's all too familiar.

The best way to deal with this is to rely on God and stay away from those who cast judgment on you as if they have a right to understand. Who made them God?

Remember, that is what Satan wants to be…God. The angels of Satan will torment us, twist things into tight balls, and cast us down to destroy us. Friends don't do that.

Satan will confuse you and everyone around you, and then he will turn everyone against each other. He doesn't care; his only desire is to drive you so crazy that you don't know the truth while remaining miserable.

Power of One Voice, LLC
Come Alive Series

5

The Mind

"Set your mind on things above, not on things on the earth." (Colossians 3:2; NKJV)

Satan will take you down if you don't prepare yourself. You might say, as I did, I'm so tired. I found myself saying that so often that I knew something was seriously wrong with my willpower. Life happens, but we cannot give up.

Having lived in a difficult childhood, I had taken on an attitude that I will not go down! I was a fighter and loved God at a very young age.

When I first saw the Word of God sitting on my mother's bookshelf (I was only seven years old), I quickly called her at work and asked her what it was. I honestly didn't know. She told me, and I told God right then and there that I would read it from cover to cover.

Little did I know it would not happen until I was in my 50s. But why? Why would it take so long? I guess I just didn't understand that it was *that important.*

I put my trust in preachers, sermons, and "religious" teachings. I read the Bible like most of us; a few verses here and a few verses there, but never did I read it from cover to cover. I knew where certain verses were, and I understood a lot of stories, but even that wasn't fully understood.

Many stories are scattered throughout God's Word. You will find snippets here and there; all the pieces are important, but reading the Bible like you would a book is vital to understanding God.

Because I promised God that I would read it from cover to cover, and I didn't for so long; I had to relook at my relationship with God and how much I had neglected it. I have come to understand that this happens to many of us.

I have also realized that I have done a huge injustice to My Awesome Father by not being interested in His Letter to me.

Yes, God wrote the WORD as a personal letter to each of us. It was to comfort, help, guide, and show how much He loved us.

Reading to understand requires diligence and true intent. It's quite a big book, and we have been told much of our lives that it's too hard for the average person to understand it. So, we just don't try.

Today we live in a world with vast help in understanding the Word. With the many translations, we can read it like a book much easier.

Challenge yourself to get busy and read, with the goal of understanding more each time. Be patient with yourself. I have found that my understanding increases each time I read, and yours will also.

I have read many translations of the Bible, and it's very interesting about the language and the clarification available. I like to pull the translations together to get a clearer understanding. Some translations are very different, but God will continue to teach you as you ask His help.

If we don't read His WORD, we tend to get unstable in our daily walk. We all need God's help; He is life's ultimate help.

This brings me to the understanding that Satan is influencing our walk from the moment we are born.

Satan tells us, *"That's not necessary,"* *"Not important,"* *"Do it later,"* *"You don't have time for that,"* etc. Satan influences our minds more than we can ever understand right now.

God does care that we know Him and has more than

surface understandings to teach us. God also wants to personally know us; while being there to guide, encourage and love us all along the way. He truly is the best friend we will ever have.

I have found that I have grown so close to God and that I don't have to be perfect by any means. All I need to be is willing to correct things that will hurt me in my walk. God wants us to have success and when you set your mind on the things of God you find that God has so much more to give you.

The Word of God is the power given to us to fully embrace who we are and what we can become as a result of accepting Salvation through the Blood of Jesus.

Unfortunately, many never get very far in their walk with God and often give up simply because they don't understand their new commitment and don't see how to get to know God.

The Bible is the go-to book for all your questions.

In **2 Corinthians 3:14,** we read;

> "But their minds were blinded. For until this day the same veil remains unlifted in the reading of the Old Testament, because the veil is taken away in Christ." (2 Corinthians 3:14; NKJV)

God's WORD Sets You Free

Here we learn how important our acceptance of Christ is *to begin* our relationship with God. If we cannot see what is necessary in order to understand God, then we are blind. By resting on the letter and shutting their eyes to the light, they became blind to the fact that the *old covenant* was abolished and done away.

Many Christians are just as blind to the same simple fact because of *the universal belief* that the 10 Commandments, including the Sabbath, are still in force. As we read in **Acts 15:1;**

> **And certain men came down from Judea and taught the brethren, "Unless you are circumcised according to the custom of Moses, you cannot be saved." (Acts 15:1; NKJV)**

The 10 Commandments were abolished when Christ came, as plainly stated in these references **(2 Corinthians 3:6-15; Galatians 3:19-25; 4:21-31; Hebrews 7:11-10:18).**

Paul specified the 10 Commandments written on stones as being abolished and done away with in **2 Corinthians 3:6-15.** I will cover this more in my next book.

There is only one way to have a sound mind: reading God's Word daily. Satan knows that whatever you get in your mind, specifically *to question things,* like in the Garden of Eden, he can work lies and make you think it's ok or allowable.

Satan confuses God's truth. Our minds must be kept healthy in order to stay away from sin.

But why the mind?

Because our mind is part of the image of God, where God communicates with us and reveals His Will to us.

We read in Colossians that we are to set our mind and keep focused habitually on the things above [the heavenly things], not on things that are on the earth [which have only temporal value].

Paul was giving instructions to put away the old way of living. He was explaining how important it was to concentrate on the eternal realities of heaven.

It was a decision to no longer trust in ritualistic observances or human work because nothing could be added to the merit of Christ's death. *His work on the cross is the only acceptable work in God's eyes.*

Paul was telling them that they now must make an ongoing decision to continually focus and set their mind on the things above.

In Romans, we read of the importance of renewing our minds with Godly values and ethical attitudes so that we may prove for ourselves what the will of God is. That which is good and acceptable and perfect in His plan and purpose for you and me is all that matters.

When we read in **Ephesians 4** of the Christian's walk, we learn the difference between a way of ignorance, not knowing, and *now* knowing.

It is written that when Jesus died and his disciples began ministering about how to walk, we would need to study and learn continually.

We are reminded that we must continually be renewed in the spirit of our mind, having a fresh, untarnished mental and spiritual attitude. And the only way is to read the original writings from God Himself found in the Holy Bible.

Books, like mine, are something you can read, but **they are not** the main source of instruction. *Always go to the Scriptures to find the "truth."* Read and prove that these are truly what God says.

I have come to understand that God has written most everything we need to know in His Word, but He wants us to search it out.

In **Proverbs 25:2** we read;

> "It is the glory of God to conceal a matter, but the glory of kings is to search out a matter." (Proverbs 25:2; NKJV)

> "It is God's privilege to conceal things and the king's privilege to discover them." (Proverbs 25:2; NLT)

We are also reminded to put on the new self, the regenerated and renewed nature, created in God's image in the righteousness and holiness of the truth.

We are to live in a way that expresses our gratitude for our salvation to God.

God renews our minds through His Truth which is the ***Word of God***.

Therefore, learning for ourselves what the truth of God is, is a necessary foundation.

If Satan can get you to believe a lie, he can begin to work in your life and eventually lead you in the direction he wants you to go.

Satan attacks the mind to gain control; therefore, we must

protect our minds from the attacks. He also attacks our emotions and gets us off course, often focusing on things we cannot control. God speaks purposely that we are not to worry but to leave things in God's hands. God knows we will have to face these kinds of distractions and give us a way out.

We read in **Philippians 4** that whatever is true, honorable, and worthy of respect, and whatever is confirmed by God's Word, to think continually on these things, centering our mind on them and implanting them in our hearts. This is solid instruction.

In **Philippians 4:9** we read;

> "The things which you learned and received and heard and saw in me, these do, and the God of peace will be with you." (Philippians 4:9; NKJV)

The verb "learned" conveys not only the concept of "increasing in intellectual knowledge" but also the idea of "learning by habitual practice."

Not only are Christians to meditate on certain things, as you read in **Philippians 4:8**. But they are to do certain things.

Christianity is very practical. It is not a dead, dry, formal, human religion of rituals, outward form, and show, but a divine, living, vital, dynamic, liberating religion.

Any religion without power to deliver men from sin, sickness, poverty, and want—now and hereafter—is not of God as you can further read here (**Matthew 7:7-11; 17:20; 21:22; Mark 9:23; 11:22-24; 16:17-18; John 14:12-15; 15:7, 16; 16:23-26; Hebrews 11; James 1**).

The mind is very powerful, and much more has been learned in recent years. Science has discovered that the mind is like a computer and can store facts and impressions, even emotions, so deep that they can be recalled many years later.

That is why trauma of the mind is so dangerous. Something can trigger a memory, and all of the sudden, it's like you are reliving it. Many who have PTSD are living in a troubled *reality by no fault of their own.*

There is an even worse danger that can affect you eternally. Satan has convinced you of lies through the feeding of the mind. Religions that preach "their way," as the only true way spoken about in the Bible, are keeping you from the truth. Religion is man's form of worshiping God, but only Salvation through Jesus can truly save you.

Your mind has been taken hostage if you believe your religion saves you. The Bible is the only source that can clear this up.

Your mind can reach into the past through memory, or it can reach into the future through imagination. And therefore, you can learn by creating opportunity and practicing the concepts that Jesus instilled in all of us.

Although we might carry scars of the past, we can also create new paths of learning when we instill good habits.

To begin this, you must let go of guilt, sorrow, and self-pity. Jesus does this for you if you accept Him.

It says in **Proverbs 23:7**;

> **"For as he thinks in his heart, so is he...." (Proverbs 23:7; NKJV)**

There is a power that is so great within you when you set your mind on the Spirit of life and peace, as we read in **Romans 8:6**;

> **"For to be carnally minded is death, but to be spiritually minded is life and peace." (Romans 8:6; NKJV)**

The same goes for setting the mind on things of the flesh, as we read in **Romans 8:5;**

> "For those who live according to the flesh set their minds on the things of the flesh, but those who live according to the Spirit, the things of the Spirit."
> (Romans 8:5; NKJV)

Satan is aware that if you set your mind on the sins or things of the flesh, you will naturally fulfill them. That is why Satan keeps your mind so occupied, so busy that you don't take authority over your habits and never find time to sit and read God's Word.

It's not just the stories you will learn, but when you read Holy Spirit sits with you and teaches you personally.

Many people, and I was one of them, become so lost in sorrow and self-pity that they become a broken record.

When I was young, I listened to all my music on a phonograph. It was a record that I bought and put on a turning wheel and then put an arm that held a needle to rest on the little grooves on that record. Whenever a groove had a tear from a scratch or possibly something spilled on it, the needle would get stuck and play the same thing repeatedly.

God's WORD Sets You Free

This is what happens in our minds. When we experience something traumatic such as a death or an experience, our mind gets stuck and thinks the same thoughts repeatedly. God lets you do what you want. He doesn't have any restraints on you. If you want to feel the same pain repeatedly, He will let you choose what you want.

However, when you decide to do more than mourn a loss or feel pain, God will help you take a new path. The most rewarding experience I ever had was when I decided to stop doing the same things repeatedly and start a new beginning.

Satan knows the tremendous power of your mind, and he tries to capture it for himself. But even more, Satan is after your thoughts and will do anything to keep you from thinking about God and His goodness.

Why? Because Satan knows that God created you special, with an identity and a destiny, he will destroy both.

Satan will get your identity so confused that you get lost, and this keeps your mind stuck where you never quite know the amazing things God created for you to accomplish. And God has more than the surface destiny for you. He purposed you to create and to go beyond.

God plants the seed, and you can nourish it to the point that it will flourish beyond your wildest dreams.

One way Satan does this is to make light of the need to read

God's Word, as I have already talked about. God's Word helps you understand the deeper reasons for everything while teaching you how much He loves you.

Proverbs 4:20-27 talks of constancy of heart and purpose, honesty in speech, the steadiness of gaze, and the right goal in your walk and in your life:

> "My son, give attention to my words; Incline your ear to my sayings. Do not let them depart from your eyes; Keep them in the midst of your heart; For they are life to those who find them, And health to all their flesh. Keep your heart with all diligence, For out of it spring the issues of life. Put away from you a deceitful mouth, And put perverse lips far from you. Let your eyes look straight ahead, And your eyelids look right before you. Ponder the path of your feet, And let all your ways be established. Do not turn to the right or the left; Remove your foot from evil." (Proverbs 4:20-27; NKJV)

The mind leads the way to our thoughts, which eventually come out through our actions. If our problems are rooted in our thinking, wouldn't it seem good to change our thoughts?

For whatever reason, *life* had trained me to judge others and to reason why they did what they did. Whether it was through

God's WORD Sets You Free

life in general or my choices, it became clear that my thoughts were taking me down the wrong road.

I needed to think differently, which was a monumental victory in my growth when I could flip things around.

When I started to remove my wrong reasoning and my judgment, I no longer had a mind full of thoughts. I freed myself and began to remember God's Word on a constant. I was amazed at how my mind was so cluttered before.

God wants us to think about good things. All through His Word, He talks about what is good and what isn't. And God is trying to educate us that what we think about, we become more of.

In **Jeremiah 4:14** it says to wash your heart from wickedness. This is a warning of the danger of evil thoughts.

> "O Jerusalem, wash your heart from wickedness, That you may be saved. How long shall your evil thoughts lodge within you? (Jeremiah 4:14; NKJV)

Jeremiah, deeply moved by God's words, expressed his sorrow and confusion to God. Jeremiah was an intercessor for the people. These people had false expectations because of the past promises of blessings, their blindness to their own sin, and the false prophets who kept telling them 'all was well.' Does this sound familiar to the times we live in?

Our thoughts do control the direction in which we walk. It's not just wicked thoughts but also the everyday things of life. If we don't purposely spend time learning and reading about God, when will we ever know what He has to say? And we will not be able to understand the deeper things which our experiences are giving an opportunity to change in our own lives as well as in the lives of those we are trying to help.

Our lives intersect with others, and God is concerned with helping all of us. We are all His children, and He wants all to return to Him. Like in the example of the body, each member affects the whole body. We are all a part of the family of God, and each experience gives opportunity to help each of us. Our choices guide us down the road of opportunity to change everything in our own paths.

In **Jeremiah 31,** the Lord says that the time is coming when I will make a new covenant with the house of Israel and Judah. God continues to bring new opportunities and new hope for change. He never gives up on us.

> "But this is the covenant that I will make with the house of Israel after those days, says the LORD: I will put My law in their minds, and write it on their hearts,

> and I will be their God, and they shall be My people."
> (Jeremiah 31:33; NKJV)

God would write His law on their hearts rather than on tablets of stone, as He did the Ten Commandments.

In **Jeremiah 17:1,** their sin was engraved on their hearts, so they wanted to disobey.

> "The sin of Judah is written with a pen of iron; with the point of a diamond it is engraved on the table of their heart, and on the horns of your altars," (Jeremiah 17:1; NKJV)

Judah's sin was written and engraved, as with a pen of iron and the point of a diamond, in two places:

1. **The table of the heart.**
2. **The horns of the altars.**

An iron chisel was used in cutting inscriptions on tables of stone, indicating the stony hearts of the people. This shows that the ancients knew the cutting power of the diamond. Not one altar of Jehovah, but the many altars to idols.

In understanding **Jeremiah 17:1**, we see how the heart reveals the true motives of each of us. This is why it's important to work on our hearts first, and only by reading God's Word can this be accomplished.

When we turn our life over to God, He, by His Holy Spirit, *builds into us the desire to obey Him.* It is a growth that happens in the heart first.

The old covenant, broken by the people, would be replaced by a new covenant. The foundation of this new covenant is Christ **(Hebrews 8:6).** It is revolutionary, involving not only Israel and Judah but even the Gentiles. It offers a unique personal relationship with God, with His laws written on individual hearts instead of stone.

Jeremiah looked forward to the day when Jesus would come to establish a permanent, personal relationship with God **(Jeremiah 29:11; 32:38-40).**

We read in **Jeremiah 29:11**;

> "For I know the thoughts that I think toward you,

> says the LORD, thoughts of peace and not of evil, to give you a future and a hope." (Jeremiah 29:11; NKJV)

God has the power to do away with the laws of nature or even with His people. But God will do neither. This is not a prediction (**Jeremiah 31:35-37**); it's a promise. This is God's way of saying that He will not reject Israel any more than He will do away with nature's laws.

I believe that God's covenants are a promise of better days to His people. He sees their struggle and stubbornness, but He wants, more than anything, to bring us all home to Him. And so, He made a new covenant.

In **Jeremiah 32:36-42** God promises restoration. After Jeremiah bought the field (**Jeremiah 32:17-25**), he began to wonder if such a move was wise. He sought relief in prayer from his nagging doubts.

In this prayer, Jeremiah affirmed that God is the Creator of heaven and earth (**Jeremiah 32:17**), the wise Judge, who is aware of our conduct (**Jeremiah 32:19**), and our Redeemer, who has great power (**Jeremiah 32:21**). God loves us and sees our situation. Whenever we doubt God's wisdom or wonder if it is practical to obey Him, we can review what we already know about Him. Such thoughts and prayers will quiet our doubts and calm our fears.

In **Jeremiah 32:35**, these pagan shrines were where the most important and grotesque part of Molech worship took place. This is where children were offered in sacrifice to this pagan god. Sound familiar? Today we are doing the same thing through many avenues. Our children have no rights; even the fetus; and yet we justify it's ok because we want our rights to do as we please.

In God's promise of restoration (**Jeremiah 32:36-42**), He uses His power to accomplish His purposes through His people.

If our will to do as we please takes the rights away from even the innocent, it doesn't serve us either.

The people of Israel had to learn that trusting God meant radically realigning their purposes and desires with His. God gave them "one heart" toward Him (**Jeremiah 32:39**). We must develop such singleness of heart and action to love God above anything else.

Remember that a covenant is a binding relationship in which God promises to bless, and His people promise to obey. God changes these things because He loves us so much and is trying to help us succeed in coming home to Him.

But also, a covenant *is a decision of the mind*; we think about what is right, we do it, and our actions reap a better relationship with God.

We can think in our minds whatever we want, but when our thoughts are not in alignment with God's thoughts, we go astray. It's just human nature.

You might think that God is not letting you do what you want. As we live in confusion with the enemy, we are likened to children, young and not knowing the dangers of the decisions we make without understanding. God is Our Father, and He doesn't want us to suffer any more than we want our own children to suffer. Following God is trusting that God knows us better than we know ourselves and always has our backs.

If you want to make your own decisions that are contrary to the guidelines God gives, then you can. God only wants the best for us. He sees far more than we do and is always trying to protect us so that we can reach the destiny path He put in us when He carefully created us before sending us to earth. That path will bring us great joy and freedom.

It's not a religious path that traps and controls us but a path that takes us to become *more* than we ever imagined. This is where faith and trust in God and His guidance catapults us at a speed we thought unimaginable.

In **Romans 2:1-11** we read about how our thoughts and actions condemn others. We pass judgment on another and yet forget we have done wrong too.

We judge from a position of arrogance or self-righteousness, but habitually, we practice the very same things we judge them for.

God asks if we think we will escape His judgment and avoid His verdict *on our* sinful lives. **Romans 2:4** encourages us "to change our mind," change our thinking. In this context, it means to reject one's sinful habits and turn to God.

> "Or do you despise the riches of His goodness, forbearance, and longsuffering, not knowing that the goodness of God leads you to repentance?" (Romans 2:4; NKJV)

God holds back His judgment in His kindness, giving people time to turn from their sins. It is easy to mistake God's patience for approval of the wrong way we are living. Self-evaluation is even more difficult, bringing ourselves to God and telling Him where we need to change.

But as Christians, we must ask God to point out our sins so that He can heal them. Unfortunately, we have often been more amazed at God's patience with others than humbled at His patience with us.

As we go through experiences, it becomes clearer that God is not *just* asking for you to "straighten up and live right," but He is saying that what you are doing, you will have to answer for on the day of judgment.

In **Romans 2:5-6** it states clearly how serious it is;

> "But in accordance with your hardness and your impenitent heart you are treasuring up for yourself wrath in the day of wrath and revelation of the righteous judgment of God, who "will render to each one according to his deeds"" (Romans 2:5-6; NKJV)

The hardness is caused by a long course of rebellion, and the impenitent heart is caused by the hardness of the heart.

In these verses, it is the storing up of things that will call for the wrath of God. The measure of wrath is varied to the extent one rejects the goodness of God, and punishment will be according to its contents. **(Romans 2:6; Matthew 11:22-24; 23:14; Revelations 20:11-15)**

So, our minds, filled with thoughts resulting in our actions towards others, are serious.

God goes on to talk about doing good.

He emphasizes what this will do for us. God wants us to see the value in doing what is right. It not only will help you personally by giving you pleasure in your heart, but it will help you draw closer to God.

Remember that God created you; therefore, the best place you could possibly end up is with God. He is what your soul longs for, but humanly we have forgotten or aren't aware of this fact. Therefore, trusting in God and doing good is going to be the best thing you could ever do for yourself.

The mind is attacked every day. And even when you are not expecting it. Satan's thoughts that he plants in *your thoughts* don't appear as a danger, but they are subtle and deceiving.

When you learn how important it is to fill your mind with God's Word, you will begin to see a difference.

The struggle you had will become less. When you speak God's Word out loud when things are troublesome, you will receive power and help from God.

The last verse I want to share, is to me, one of the most clearly written instructions on the subject of the mind and what we think about.

I found great victory in reading this and utilizing its wisdom. I purposely would think these things and when fear overcame me, I would recite this verse out loud to myself.

> "And now, dear brothers and sisters, one final thing. Fix your thoughts on what is true and honorable, and right, and pure, and lovely, and admirable. Think about things that are excellent and worthy of praise. Keep putting into practice all you learned and received from me—everything you heard from me and saw me doing. Then the God of peace will be with you." (Philippians 4:8-9; NLT)

What we put into our mind determines what comes out in our words and actions. Paul tells us to program our mind with thoughts that are true, honorable, right, pure, lovely, admirable, excellent, and worthy of praise. Do you have problems with impure thoughts; do you have anger issues?

Examine what you are putting into your mind through television, the internet, books, conversations, movies, and whom you hang out with. Replace harmful input with wholesome material. Above all, spend quality time reading God's Word and praying. Ask God to help you focus on what is good and pure. It takes intentional living practices by implementing new habits that will change everything in your life.

Keep in mind that it is not enough to hear or read the Word of God or even to know it well. We must also put it into practice. How easy it is to listen to a sermon and forget the things we heard. Put the things you hear into action in your life, and you will experience why God's principles bring peace and joy.

All through the Bible, men and women struggled with each other. The stories are many but the message of God is the same.

Be careful of what you put in your mind because what you think begins to form a path that eventually controls you.

In the Old Testament, God often referred to David as a man after His own heart. But David's thoughts of Bathsheba led him down a road where he suffered greatly in his life with guilt and wrongdoing.

David's sin was born in his mind first, and then his thoughts took over until he acted on it.

Anyone of us can take a wrong road if we are not careful with how we think and what we do. But there is a simple solution that can stop you and make you think.

Commit to reading, studying and praying every day and this will be your armor against your human tendencies.

May God help us all stay close to Him.

6

"The Mind" Study

FURTHER STUDY

Keep Your Mind Set on God

Mind of the Lord

Who of the natural men that live in the carnal passions can know the mind of the Lord that he may instruct the spiritual man?

Fill in the blanks.

> "For who has _____ the mind of the _____ that he may instruct Him? But _____ have the _____ of Christ." (1 Corinthians 2:16; NKJV)

This verse says that our victory will come when we set our minds on the same things Christ did.

And when you accept Jesus as Lord and Savior of your life, then you will have the same Spirit. Holy Spirit becomes your power to live in this world.

Mind of Man

Please read **1 Chronicle 22:7-10 (NKJV)** to answer the questions below.

> "And David said to Solomon: "My son, as for me, it was in my mind to build a house to the name of the LORD my God; but the word of the LORD came to me, saying, 'You have shed much blood and have made great wars; you shall not build a house for My name, because have shed much blood on the earth in My sight. 'Behold, a son shall be born to you, who shall be a man of rest; and I will give him rest from all his enemies all around. His name shall be Solomon, for I will give peace and quietness to Israel in his days. He shall build a house for My name, and he shall be My son, and I will be his Father, and I will establish the throne of his kingdom over Israel forever.'" (1 Chronicles 22:7-10; NKJV)

God's WORD Sets You Free

Why was David not directed by God to build a house to the name of the LORD my God?

_____
_____

What does this say about the mind of man vs. the mind of God?

_____
_____

How are we to know what the mind of God is instructing us? Where do we find the answers as we spend time with Him?

_____
_____

Mind Stayed on God

Please read and fill in the blanks for the following verse.

> "You will _____ him in perfect peace, Whose _____ is stayed on You _____ he trusts in You." (Isaiah 26:3; NKJV)

This is a promise for all men of all ages who keep their minds on God and who trust in Him at all times, in all things, and in all places.

In **Psalm 91** we understand that our safety comes in abiding (dwelling) in the Presence of God. The Hebrew word used for "dwells" in **Psalm 91:1** means to sit down, to dwell; to remain; to settle in the sense of taking up a homestead or staking out a claim and resisting all claim-jumpers; to possess a place and live on it.

4 things God is to those in the secret place and under His shadow?
(Psalm 91:2)

1._____

2._____

3._____

4._____

Anxious Mind

When we seek the things of God, we become different in many things. We lose the fear and the need to put others down. We focus on our relationship with God.

In **Luke 12:29-30 (NKJV)**, please fill in the blanks.

> "And do not seek what you should _____ or what you should _____, nor have an anxious mind. For all these things the nations of the world seek after, and your Father _____ that you _____ these things."

Let seeking of necessities be secondary. Spend first energies in seeking God and His righteousness; these things will be added as we read in **Luke 12:31** and **Matthew 6:33**.

A Carnal Mind is Enmity against God.

Romans 8:6-7; NKJV; Please fill in the blanks.

> "For to be carnally minded is _____, but to be

> spirituality minded is _____ and _____. Because the carnal mind is _____ against God; for it is not subject to _____, nor indeed can be." (Romans 8:6-7; NKJV)

Those who set their affections on the sins of the flesh will naturally fulfill them. When it ceases to rebel, then it ceases to sin.

As long as it lives in rebellion, it cannot please God.

You can live a sinless life if you want to. Staying close to the Word and living according to God is vital. Your victory comes from what you set your mind to.

Never believe that you don't have the ability or the authority to live righteously. God will give you the strength and honor you desire.... Ask Him for His help and get busy studying the WORD daily.

The Mind God Gives ALL

Finding a place in God's Word where He clarifies the kind of mind He put in us is a wonderful discovery.

In a world where self-discovery, self-awareness and self-empowerment often rules humans at high speeds, we all wonder about it.

If we are capable of so much more than what "organized religion" has indoctrinated us, it's no wonder we want to break out of the box of legalism. Even if your church isn't specifically categorized as strict legalism, you will find yourself stuck and dissatisfied if they don't teach the power of what God has created us to become.

In my next book I will cover this more in depth but for now let's look at the surface of just who we are and why our minds are created to rule and reign.

In **2 Timothy 1:7**:

> "For God has not given us a spirit of fear, but of power and of love and of a sound mind." (2 Timothy 1:7; NKJV)

In **vs 6** we learn how important it is to stir up the gift of God which is in us.

4 Things the Gift Consists of:

1. **Spirit of boldness** (v. 7; Romans 8:15).

In **Romans 8:15** what did we NOT receive; what are we freed from when saved from sin?

_____

2. Spirit of power (v 7; Luke 24:49; John 14:12; Acts 1:8; 1 Corinthians 16:10; 1 Timothy 4:14).

In **Luke 24:49** what will we be endued with from on high?

_____

In this verse the Greek word for power is *dunamis* which means inherent power; the power of reproducing itself. This type of power implies need of constant activity and use for continued reproduction. From the word dunamis we get dynamo and dynamics – the branch of mechanics related to motion, the principles of active operation. Just as a dynamo needs to be in motion to produce power, one needs to stir up the gift of God into his life **(v 6; 1 Timothy 4:14).**

3. Spirit of love (v 7; 1 Corinthians 13:4).

In **1 Corinthians 13:4** we read about God's kind of love of which we receive opportunity to embody.

God's WORD Sets You Free

What 5 things describe this kind of love in 1 Corinthians 13:4?

1. _____
2. _____
3. _____
4. _____
5. _____

4. Spirit of a sound mind, understanding, and judgment (v 7; Galatians 5:22-23).

In **Galatians 5:22-23** we are reminded of the fruit of the Holy Spirit; it is the only sure way to have peace while living on earth.

Name the 9 Fruits of the Spirit

1. _____

2. _____

3. _____

4. _____

5. _____

6. _____

7. _____

8. _____

9. _____

Power of One Voice, LLC
Come Alive Series

7

Living by Faith

"Now faith is the substance of things hoped for, the evidence of things not seen. **(Hebrews 11:1; NKJV)**

The beginning point of faith is believing in God's character: *He is whom He says.* The end point is believing in God's promises: *He will do what He says.*

We demonstrate true faith when we believe that God will fulfill His promises even though we don't see those promises materializing yet. **(John 20:24-31)**

Faith is a word with many meanings. It can mean *"faithfulness"* **(Matthew 24:45)**. It can mean *"absolute trust,"* as shown by some of the people who came to Jesus for healing **(Luke 7:2-10)**.

It can mean *"confident hope"* **(Hebrews 11:1).** Or, as James points out, it can even mean a *"barren belief"* that does not result in good deeds **(James 2:14-26).**

When someone claims to have faith, what he or she may have is intellectual assent or agreement with a set of Christian teachings. These would be considered incomplete faith.

True faith transforms our conduct as well as our thoughts. If our life remains unchanged, we don't truly believe the truths we claim to believe.

James 2:18, at first glance, this verse seems to contradict **Romans 3:28**, "We are made right with God through faith and not by obeying the law." But deeper investigation shows that the teachings of James and Paul are not at odds.

While it is true that our good deeds can never earn salvation, true faith always results in a changed life and good deeds. Paul speaks against those who try to be saved by deeds instead of true faith. James speaks against those who confuse mere intellectual assent with true faith. After all, even demons know who Jesus is, but they don't obey him **(James 2:19).** True faith involves a commitment of your whole self to God.

We must be careful to understand faith as Paul uses the word because he ties faith closely to salvation. It is not something we must *do* in order to earn salvation—if that were true, then faith would be just one more *deed*, and Paul clearly states that human deeds can never save us **(Galatians 2:15-16)**.

If observing the Jewish laws cannot justify us, why should we still obey the Ten Commandments and other Old Testament laws?

We know that Paul was not saying the law is bad because in another letter, he wrote, "The law itself is holy, and its commands are holy and right and good" **(Romans 7:12)**. Instead, he is saying that the law can never make us acceptable to God.

The law still has an important role to play in the life of a Christian. The law guards us against sin by giving us standards for behavior; and convicts us of sin, leaving us the opportunity to ask for God's forgiveness.

The law also drives us to trust in the sufficiency of Christ because we can never keep the Ten Commandments perfectly. The law cannot save us but guides us to live as God desires.

In **Galatians, 2:4-5** Paul answers about the so-called false Christians secretly brought in. These false Christians were most likely from the party of the Pharisees **(Acts 15:5)**. These were the strictest religious leaders of Judaism, some of whom had been converted.

We don't know if these were representatives of well-meaning converts or those trying to pervert Christianity. Most commentators agree that neither Peter nor James had any part in this conspiracy.

> "Even that question came up only because of some so-called Christians there – false ones really – who were secretly brought in. They sneaked in to spy on us and take away the freedom we have in Christ Jesus. They wanted to enslave us and force us to follow their Jewish regulations. But we refused to give in to them for a single moment. We wanted to preserve the truth of the gospel message for you." (Galatians 2:4-5; NLT)

We normally think of taking a stand against those who might lead us into immoral behavior, but Paul had to take a hard line against the most moral people. We must not give in to those who make keeping man-made standards a condition for salvation, even when such people are morally upright or in respected positions.

The fact is that faith is a gift God gives us because He is saving us **(Ephesians 2:8)**. It is God's grace, not our faith, that saves us. In His mercy, however, when He saves us, He gives us Faith—a relationship with His Son that helps us become like Him.

Through the faith He gives us, He carries us from death into life **(1 John 5:24)**.

When you read the life of Abraham in **Genesis 12-25**, you understand that all God did, He did in order to perfect Abraham's *faith*.

Faith is a spiritual principle, and when we learn to have faith while living on earth, we build a greater understanding of its importance through what we experience.

Matthew 9:29 explains that it shall be done to you according to your faith.

> "Then He touched their eyes, saying, "According to your faith let it be to you." (Matthew 9:29; NKJV)

When God works in our lives, it is always in response to faith. What hinders the working of God is not His lack of power but *our lack of faith*.

James 1:5-6 says this about faith;

> "If any of you lacks wisdom, let him ask of God, who gives to all liberally and without reproach, and it will be given to him. But let him ask in faith, with no

> **doubting, for he who doubts is like a wave of the sea driven and tossed by the wind." (James 1:5-6; NKJV)**

By "wisdom," James is talking about knowledge and the ability to make wise decisions in difficult circumstances.

We can pray to God whenever we need wisdom, and He will generously supply what we need.

Christians don't have to grope around in the dark, hoping to stumble upon answers. We can ask for God's wisdom to guide our choices.

Then James talks about the importance of believing and not wavering. We must believe not only in the existence of God but also in ***His loving care.***

This includes relying on God and expecting that He will hear and answer when we pray.

We must put away our critical attitude when we come to Him. God doesn't grant every thoughtless or selfish request. We must have confidence that God will align our desires with His purposes.

Everything we lack is because we don't understand that God wants us to have it. God wants His children to have everything they need in order to have *abundant life*; we just need to ask for it and believe He will give it.

This brings us an understanding of how **Great our God is.**

If you get into your car in the morning, turn the ignition, and head to work, you forget that you had a belief that took you to your car in the first place. Why would you get all ready for work, with every detail taken care of to be gone for the day from your home, lock the house with lunch in hand and beautifully dressed for the day, if you didn't have a belief that you had the ability to get to work or anywhere else?

We take for granted all the things we do daily that require faith to accomplish our goals. If God has given you this basis for fulfilling your personal goals, don't you think it will work the same way as believing in Him to help you?

Satan wants us to think we are victims and have no control, we can't do anything for ourselves, and we just have to wait for the right time if we want something from God. That is hogwash!!! Ask, and you shall receive.

There is a law on this earth of seed and harvest. What you plant, you will sow and reap. God has always wanted you to understand that you do have the power to progressively grow in your daily life.

A lot of our problems in life are the result of our choices.

Choose better and reap a more productive harvest; this is God's desire for you.

God is trying to get us to understand that having faith must be connected to believing that God can do all things.

In order to have more faith, we must understand first why we must have more.

Let's look at **Matthew 8:13**;

> "Then Jesus said to the centurion, "Go your way; and as you have believed, so let it be done for you." And his servant was healed that same hour." (Matthew 8:13; NKJV)

This story is also found in **Luke 7:1-10**. When Jesus saw the faith of the Roman officer, he used this story to mirror the kind of faith we all should have.

Sometimes we are too close to "following" everything as *we think* it should be and forget the most important things that can drive us forward; seeing God and His intent for us in the first place.

> "When Jesus heard these things, He marveled at him and turned around and said to the crowd that followed Him, "I say to you, I have not found such great faith not even in Israel!" (Luke 7:9; NKJV)

Matthew 8:5 says the Roman officer visited Jesus, while **Luke 7:3** says he sent Jewish elders to present his request to Jesus. In those days, dealing with a person's messengers was the same as dealing with the one who had sent them. Thus, in dealing with the messengers, Jesus was dealing with the officer.

For his Jewish audience, Matthew emphasized the Roman soldier's faith. For his Gentile audience, Luke highlighted the good relationship between the Jewish elders and the Roman officer.

The Roman officer didn't come to Jesus, and he didn't expect Jesus to come to him. Just as this officer did not need to be present to have his orders carried out, Jesus didn't need to be present to heal.

The officer's faith was especially amazing because he was a Gentile who had not been raised to know a loving God.

And in **Matthew 9:29,** we read;

> "Then He touched their eyes saying, "According to your faith let it be to you." (Matthew 9:29; NKJV)

Jesus didn't respond immediately to the blind men's pleas. He waited to see if they had faith. Not everyone who says he wants help believes God can help him. Jesus may have waited and questioned these men to emphasize and increase their faith.

When you think that God is too slow in answering your prayers, consider that He might be testing you as He did the blind man. Do you believe that God can help you? Do you want His help?

In this story of the blind man, they were persistent. They went right into the house where Jesus was staying. They knew Jesus could heal them, and they would let nothing stop them from finding Him. That's real faith in action.

If you believe Jesus is the answer to your every need, don't let anything or anyone stop you from reaching out to Him.

Matthew 13:58 says He did not do many miracles in Nazareth because of their unbelief.

But how can we know that we are living by faith and not because it seems "right" to do it? How can we know that our decisions are driven by God and not by Satan and his demonic powers?

We can ask ourselves some things that can help us know we are walking by faith.

First, ask yourself whether you are doing this for the glory of God or just to please yourself. When Abraham was told he would be the father of many nations and he knew he and his wife were too old to have children, it says in **Romans 4:20** that *with respect to the promise of God*, Abraham did not waver in unbelief but grew strong in faith, giving glory to God.

Trusting God when it's the hardest and when it seems so impossible is when you find that you don't just have faith in faith, but you have faith in God.

Many say, "Just keep the faith," or "Have faith, and everything will work for good." But faith in what? Is this the world's way to leave God out and simply say to have faith in faith? I'm afraid it is Satan's way of steering clear of God altogether.

Abraham and Sarah, although the story reveals a lot of struggles, trusted God, and God performed the miraculous. Because Abraham knew God, he had assurance that He was also able to perform what was promised.

But Abraham had learned about God through his *relationship and walk*. His motivation to trust God came from his desire to give God the glory in all things.

Abraham was just like any man, but what he became after his walk with God reveals that he changed *from within.*

Abraham learned what faith does and why learning about having it is important. Faith in God always gives glory to God.

Everything we have is because God has given it to us. But humans tend to carry the "entitlement mentality." They fight with each other to have what another has. We give ourselves way too much credit for what we have. God has given, but we can lose what we have if we choose to live wrong and against God's ways.

Abraham saw the frailty of his own life and the promise God had given him. He had no idea how he would be the father of so many. Both his wife and himself, so old, far beyond the child-bearing years, all he could do was give it to God and trust Him.

This was a special story in that the hidden message from God was for Abraham to simply give God his life. True faith, which God longs to see in all of us, is motivated *only by the desire to glorify God.*

Secondly, are you willing to wait if things take time and if faith must take root? Or are you going to make it happen one way or another?

Consider the costly pearl waiting in the oyster bed for a moment. *The longer it waited, the more valuable it became.*

True faith is not in a hurry until God opens the way.

Trusting that God has our back, that God wants good things for His children, and that He knows what's best brings us a greater understanding of how much God cares for us.

When we impatiently rush ahead of the Lord, we act on our fleshly unbelief, thinking we know what's best. It says in Romans that whatever is not from faith is a sin.

God wants us to have faith and to experience what having faith does to us from within. He will not force it on us, and He may not explain what it will do for us because He wants us to *experience it* for ourselves.

Thirdly, can we defend our actions from what God's Word says? True faith is grounded in the Word of God, as is stated in Romans. Faith comes by hearing and hearing by the Word of Christ.

As you do what you want to do, no matter how reasonable or safe it may seem, does it contradict God's teachings in His Word?

As you learn what God says about how to live your life among others, you must ask yourself if you are violating any of His principles.

God's WORD Sets You Free

It might seem ok to hurt another when they have hurt you or to prove your way is "right," but God is asking you to not act out of human nature but to give God the glory by *doing what's right.*

Our friends might encourage us, and we might be able to justify our actions, but God is looking to do something for you beyond the petty quarrels of this life.

After you have proven to *trust God and do right,* there is more God wants to teach you. And it's good!

God wants to bless you but cannot do this if you continue to *reason* and obey your human nature by hurting others.

If you know what the Word says and you are justifying your actions by hurting someone as they hurt you, then God will allow you to do what you want.

He will wait for another opportunity if one comes along.

The ***fourth and last*** question you should ask yourself is how you feel. Do you have true peace and joy about what you are about to do?

After my first time reading the Bible from cover to cover, I realized how much God loves all and how little I knew about Him.

Knowing God's Word on everything brings lasting peace and joy.

Colossians 3:15 says.

> "And let the peace of God rule in your hearts, to which also you were called in one body; and be thankful." (Colossians 3:15; NKJV)

Christians should live in peace. To live in peace does not mean that suddenly all differences of opinion are eliminated, but it does require that loving Christians work together despite their differences.

Love is not a feeling but a decision to meet others' needs **(1 Corinthians 13).** To clothe ourselves with love leads to peace between individuals and among the members of the body of Christ.

The word rule comes from the language of athletics. Paul tells us to let Christ's peace be the umpire or referee in our hearts. Our heart is the center of conflict because our feelings and desires clash – our fears and hopes, distrust and trust, jealousy and love struggle within us. Paul explains that to deal with these constant conflicts and live as God wants, we must decide between conflicting elements by using the rule of peace.

God's WORD Sets You Free

Trying to find myself after years of not understanding the Word of God, I had no peace within. I wanted peace, oh how I wanted peace. However, I didn't trust because of the struggles of life I had endured.

Today, I fully trust God with my life and His Will. I love God and understand His love for me in ways I never thought possible.

As we each step out in faith, we will experience human fears and anxieties. If we walk in faith and learn daily of God's Word, these fears will eventually be overcome by a deeper joy and peace in God. This is how Holy Spirit works in response to our faith in God's Word.

Unfortunately, we all have lacked faith many times in our lives. It's part of the earthly journey to battle against things not of God.

As I look back, I see how I fell into the human traps where I trusted either in myself, other humans, or other belief systems, but the good thing is now I understand why.

I fell into these things because I was not walking daily directly with God in His Word. I knew of verses that were powerful, but I didn't have daily time to sit and study to know what God has to say.

Honestly, this lack was something I am responsible for. We

cannot blame religions for things we are responsible for, but when we don't know any better, that is when God's Instruction Book, The Bible, comes in handy.

Religions that teach erroneously, not solely what God is teaching, are seriously held accountable, and they lead many people astray. And those who do not teach the Salvation message *correctly and don't instruct all to give their lives to Jesus* are seriously in error. The death on the cross, the Blood of Jesus, is the beginning of our walk.

I believe that God allowed me to walk and experience many things in order for me to understand deeper His saving grace, His love, and His perfect way.

I experienced the highs and lows and the ultimate demise of my own self. But God saved me repeatedly, and it is to God I give all the glory.

Life is hard for so many, but what's important is how God can still transform us and make us new no matter what we go thru.

God is greater, and He will always provide a way back to Him.

Satan will weaken us and discourage our faith by tempting us to stop trusting in God.

God's WORD Sets You Free

The only way to victory in this life is to walk with Him, side by side, learning of Him daily from His Word.

When we seek God's glory and learn why we wait on Him, we begin to experience the joy that surpasses all our understanding.

God wants you to willingly come with Him. He will not drag you by the hair, screaming and yelling, but He wants you to want a relationship with Him.

Please make a new commitment to find out everything in God's Word and go to the Word itself to do this.

8

"Living By Faith" Study

Further Study

Faith's Worship

In **Hebrews 11:4,** we read about Abel's faith:

> "By faith Abel offered to God a more excellent sacrifice than Cain, through which he obtained witness that he

God's WORD Sets You Free

> was righteous, God testifying of his gifts; and through it he being dead still speaks." (Hebrews 11:4; NKJV)

How did Abel offer to God a more excellent sacrifice? Abel offered by _____

Of Abel's sacrifice and his being dead for a long time, what do his actions do for us today?

_____
_____

In **Genesis 4:4**, What did Abel bring?

_____

In **Genesis 4:3**, What did Cain bring?

_____
_____

In **Genesis 4:5**, How did God feel about Cain's offering, and how did Cain react?

_____
_____

Like us today, Cain and Abel became responsible for acting in personal faith.

Cain's sacrifice was brought in as a result of self-will and unbelief of the importance of the blood. He did something to *appease* God without acknowledging guilt or faith and ignored why the "blood" was paramount.

Cain's anger was without excuse as we learn in **v 6**, for God still offered to accept the right sacrifice, as we read in **v 7**.

Cain offered *his own idea* of what was good and right, the offering of the ground. *Cain ignored his own sinfulness and personal need of God.* Why do you think God wants us to do things a certain way?

_____
_____
_____

Like in school, learning something takes steps to get to a higher understanding. Doing things God's Way can help you understand, but in what way? Explain your own thoughts.

_____
_____
_____
_____

In **Genesis 4:13-14** we see the first recorded remorse of Cain:

> "And Cain said to the LORD, "My punishment is greater than I can bear! Surely You have driven me out this day from the face of the ground; I shall be hidden from Your face; I shall be a fugitive and a vagabond on the earth, and it will happen that anyone who finds me will kill me." (Genesis 4:13-14; NKJV)

By now, Adam had been on earth for about 130 years **(4:25; 5:3)**. At a very moderate rate of increase; there could have been about 500,000 people by this time. Cain himself built a city which would require many people **(4:17)**. Every son of man had sons and daughters and started branches of the race **(4:15-24; 5:1-32; 6:1-2)**.

In **Genesis 4:15** we see God's Divine Intervention similar to **Genesis 3:21** where God provided them with clothing.

> "And the LORD said to him, "Therefore, whoever kills Cain, vengeance shall be taken on him sevenfold." And the LORD set a mark on Cain, lest anyone finding him should kill him." (Genesis 4:15; NKJV)

The mark is translated from the Hebrew word, *owth*, which means token or sign. The idea is that God gave him a pledge that vengeance would be taken sevenfold on anyone who became his murderer. It was not a physical mark or a change of color. No specific race began with Cain. All his line perished in the flood **(Genesis 6:8, 18; 7:1)**. All races as we know them now began after Noah **(10:1-32)**.

What is amazing to understand about this fact that Cain was worried he would be killed; is to read that God still put around him a deterent if anyone would attempt it. Vengeance shall be taken on him sevenfold as we read Genesis 4:15. God is awesome!

__Faith's Walk__

In **Hebrews 11:5** we read:

> "By faith Enoch was taken away so that he did not see death, "and was not found, because God had taken him"; for before he was taken he had this testimony, that he pleased God." (Hebrews 11:5; NKJV)

In **Hebrew 11:5,** we read about Enoch. What happened to Enoch? And what was his testimony?

_____
_____
_____

Who had taken Enoch? **(also see Genesis 5:24)**

_____
_____

How long did Enoch live? **(Genesis 5:23)**

_____
_____

In **Genesis 5:22**, the Hebrew word used to explain the type of walk Enoch had was *halak*. It means to walk up and down and be conversant. Enoch and Noah were the only antediluvians (belonging to the ages before the Biblical Flood of Noah, the second flood) who walked with God **(Genesis 5:22; 6:9)**.

Abel, Enoch, and Noah are the only ones referred to as being godly during this age **(Genesis 4:4; 5:22; 7:1; Luke 17:26-27; Hebrews 11:1-7; I Peter 3:20; 2 Peter 2:4-5; Jude 14)**

In **Hebrews 11:6,** we see the absolute necessity of faith and the secret of pleasing God. Look up this verse in the NKJV and fill in the blanks:

> "But without _____ it is impossible to _____ Him, for he who comes to _____ must _____ that He is, and that He is a rewarder of those who _____ seek Him."
> (Hebrews 11:6; NKJV)

Faith's Work

In **Hebrews 11:7,** we learn about Noah's active preservation of faith that took place.

> "By faith Noah, being divinely warned of things not yet seen, moved with godly fear, prepared an ark for the saving of his household, by which he condemned the world and became heir of the righteousness which is according to faith." (Hebrews 11:7; NKJV)

God's WORD Sets You Free

What was Noah warned by God about?
_____
_____

What moved Noah to act?
_____
_____

When Noah prepared the ark, what message did this send to the world?
_____
_____

(also see: Genesis 6:8-8:19; 1 Peter 3:20)

"By _____ Noah, being _____ warned of things not yet _____, moved with godly fear, _____ an ark for the _____ of his household, by which he condemned the world and became _____ of the righteousness which is according to _____." (Hebrews 11:7; NKJV)

Faith's Obedience

In **Hebrews 11:8-10** we read:

> "By faith Abraham obeyed when he was called to go out to the place which he would receive as an inheritance. And he went out, not knowing where he was going. By faith he dwelt in the land of promise as in a foreign country, dwelling in tents with Isaac and Jacob, the heirs with him of the same promise; for he waited for the city which has foundations, whose builder and maker is God." (Hebrews 11:8-10; NKJV)

How did Abraham go, walk, and obey God?

_____
_____

Why did Abraham go? Did God call him? Or did he just decide to move?

_____
_____

God's WORD Sets You Free

What did God promise to give Abraham?

_____

_____

(Genesis 15:18)

> "By _____ he dwelt in the land of promise as in a foreign _____, dwelling in tents with Isaac and Jacob, the _____ with him of the same _____; for he _____ for the city which has _____, whose builder and maker is _____." (Hebrews 11:9-10; NKJV)

In **Hebrews 11:10**, Abraham waited for a permanent dwelling; what specifically was that place?

_____

_____

(see Hebrews 11:13-16)

Faith's Reckoning

Sarah experienced life-giving faith. In the story of Sarah, it is here that we see "true faith" *as counting things that do not exist as though they did.* This is what God exercised when He called the world into existence. **(Hebrews 11:3; 2 Peter 3:5; Genesis 1:1; Job 38:4-7)**

In **Hebrews 11:11; NKJV** (fill in the blanks):

> "By _____ Sarah herself also received _____ to *conceive* seed, and she bore a child when she was past the age, because she *judged* Him _____ who had _____." (Hebrews 11:11; NKJV)

In the verse above **(Hebrews 11:11)**, the *italicized words* have a new understanding when referring to the Greek word used in writing the scripture.

The Greek word *katabole* to describe "conceive" means casting

God's WORD Sets You Free

down. The idea is not only to conceive but to bring forth. The Greek word *hegeomai* to describe "judged" means to esteem. When you don't know the original Greek, you can easily be confused by what is translated into English.

What did Sarah's husband do when God said she would give him a son?
_____
_____

(Genesis 17:15-17; NKJV)

What did Sarah do when God revealed that she would bare a son?
_____
_____

(Genesis 21:1-7; NKJV)

How did God deal with Sarah's reaction?
_____
_____

(Genesis 18:14-15)

Was Abraham's laughter the same as Sarah's? How was it different?

_____

_____

(John 8:56; NKJV)

The Greek word used to describe "rejoiced" is *agalliao*. It describes that Abraham *rejoiced exceedingly*.

God told Abraham what to name the son that Sarah would bear. What was his name?

_____

_____

(Genesis 17:19; NKJV)

His name would mean *laughter*.

When you see that the name God told them to give their son means *laughter*, you realize that God understood their reaction, didn't condemn them but enjoyed it. Enjoyed it the same way that you might hear your toddler say funny things. In some ways the name of Isaac and the meaning would remind them and us of the story throughout the ages. The story is paramount in how *God's true nature is*. God loved them, understood them and accepted their reaction.

God's WORD Sets You Free

God understands all of us and is not the judgmental...ready to condemn us...Father as *Satan has tried to portray Him* since the garden in Genesis. God is an awesome, loving, gentle, kind Father who wants to sit with us, guide us and love us. God shared in naming Isaac that *He is* fun, and loves a good laugh.

Through this story, I took on a new picture of our Heavenly Father and His genuine humor watching His children even as they struggle to take on His nature of faith. He knows it's not easy but He will help us and with a loving hand.

Sarah reckoned or counted God to be true to His Word, as we read in **Hebrews 11:11**.

> "Therefore from one man, and him as good as dead, were born as many as the stars of the sky in multitude - innumerable as the sand which is by the seashore." (Hebrews 11:12; NKJV)

How many would be born as a result of Sarah bearing this son? Describe as God does, in **Hebrews 11:12, NKJV**.

_____

_____

The heavenly hope given by God to encourage His children

how to act when waiting on the promises is found in **Hebrews 11:13-16**. This is something we must put into action into our own lives.

> "These all died in faith, not having received the promises, but having seen them afar off were assured of them, embraced them and confessed that they were strangers and pilgrims on the earth. For those who say such things declare plainly that they seek a homeland. And truly if they had called to mind that country from which they had come out, they would have had opportunity to return. But now they desire a better, that is, a heavenly country. Therefore God is not ashamed to be called their God, for He has prepared a city for them." (Hebrews 11:13-16; NKJV)

How do we see things in faith? Are things close and touchable? One word that describes the distance and the same word used in the story of when Jesus met the ten lepers. (**v 13; Luke 17:12**)

_____

Those who died in faith; died without a true experience of the

God's WORD Sets You Free

promises but they saw things in their "belief" afar off and put into action three things. What were they? **(v 13)**

1. _____

2. _____

3. _____

Those that say such things declare plainly that they seek what? **(v 14)**

_____

What did they desire? **(v 16)**

_____

Power of One Voice, LLC
Come Alive Series

9

When Satan Goes to Church

"For as I was passing through and considering the objects of your worship, I even found an altar with this inscription: TO THE UNKNOWN GOD. Therefore, the One whom you worship without knowing, Him I proclaim to you: "God, who made the world and everything in it, since He is Lord of heaven and earth, does not dwell in temples made with hands. Nor is He worshiped with men's hands, as though He needed anything, since He gives to all life, breath, and all things."
(Acts 17:23-25; NKJV)

Paul came on the scene in **Acts 17**, entering a Jewish

synagogue as was his custom. For three Sabbaths, he engaged in discussion and friendly debate with them from the Scriptures.

He explained and pointed out scriptural evidence that it was necessary for Christ to suffer and rise from the dead. He told them that Jesus, whom he was proclaiming to them, is the Christ, the Anointed, the Messiah.

Paul found that some were persuaded to believe and joined Paul and Silas, along with many God-fearing Greeks and leading women.

But it was the unbelieving Jews that became jealous, and taking along some thugs from the low-life's in the marketplace, they formed a mob and set the city in an uproar.

Paul then went into a Jewish synagogue at Berea and found people more noble and open-minded than those in Thessalonica.

They received the message of salvation through faith in Christ with great eagerness, examining the Scriptures daily to see if these things were so.

As a result, many of them became believers, together with a number of prominent Greek women and men.

But...

Once again, the Jews of Thessalonica learned that the word of God concerning eternal salvation through faith in Christ had also been preached by Paul at Berea. They came there, too, agitating and disturbing the crowds once again.

Then Paul was at Athens, and while waiting for Timothy and Silas to rejoin him, Paul's spirit was greatly angered when he saw that the city was full of idols.

So, he had new discussions in the synagogue with the Jews and the God-fearing Gentiles and in the marketplace day after day with any who happened to be there.

Then Epicurean and Stoic philosophers began to engage in conversation with him. Some called him an idle babbler with his eclectic, scrap-heap learning.

Others said he seems to be a proclaimer of strange deities because he was preaching the good news about Jesus and the resurrection.

Then they took Paul to the Areopagus Hill of Ares, the Greek god of war, and asked *their god* about this man and his strange teachings.

They also told *their god* that he (*their god*) was bringing to light many new understandings. Keep in mind that this was where the court was held concerning questions of religion and morals.

In Athens, the gospel message was examined by the supposed experts of philosophy and religion.

So now we come to the verse I shared at the beginning of this chapter.

Standing in the center of Areopagus, Mars Hill, Paul said: "Men of Athens, I observe with every turn I make throughout the city that you are very religious and devout in all respects."

This is where although Paul observed *their devout religious acts* were noticed, he made a point to tell them it did not bring glory to God.

Then Paul reminded them of the greatness of God and how God planned all along that man would eventually seek Him and find Him, though He is never very far from us.

And so, we see Paul's struggle with religion vs. knowing God. Nothing is new. We still deal with the same shrouds of secrecy in religion vs. true honesty, sincere love, and devotion to God's love and way.

I ask you to ask yourself, do you want religion, or do you want to know God and begin to learn, study and pray to God?

Religion is seen in the Bible, but those who had a heart of sincerely worshiping Almighty God, the one and only God, spoke to God's heart. God knew them by their hearts.

Satan will always be in the church as long as this world awaits the return of Christ. And even when Jesus came, there are many references where he interacted with them.

It was the *religions* that killed Jesus as they joined with the world forces. And so, we see that nothing has changed.

Jesus cast out demons in the synagogue, and Paul wrote to believers to warn them about Satan and his devices.

In **Acts 5,** we read of the fate of Ananias and Sapphira. The sin Ananias and Sapphira committed was not stinginess or holding back part of the money. God gives us the choice whether or not to sell the land and how much to give.

Their sin was lying to God and God's people, saying they gave the whole amount but holding back some for themselves and trying to make themselves *appear* more generous than they really were. This act was judged harshly because dishonesty, greed, and covetousness are destructive in a church, preventing the Holy Spirit from working effectively.

All lying is bad, but when we lie to try to deceive God and His people about our relationship with Him; we destroy our testimony for Christ.

Remember that Satan is the father of lies, as we read in **John**

8:44. When Ananias and Sapphira deliberately lied, they took the moral character of the one behind all lies, the devil himself.

Remember that Satan knows that outside the church (not just the organized churches but also the hearts), people are living *as they chose*, so they are not a threat to the message of Jesus but inside is where Satan wants to be. He wants to cause trouble in the hearts and churches trying to fellowship and love Jesus. And the Bible clearly states that Satan easily disguises himself as a servant of righteousness.

Remember Saul of Tarsus. He thought he was doing the will of God when he opposed the church. But in reality he was doing the will of Satan.

Satan has agents in the pew, and scripture refers to them as false brethren and apostles. I am not trying to keep you from worshiping in a church but be careful of religions that slowly get you to do things according to their ideas. Always use God's Word to know what God wants.

God wants you to have fellowship, so finding a Bible-preaching church is good, but keep reading the Word for yourself so that God can teach you personally.

The parable of the tares teaches that Satan has "children" and that he sows them wherever God sows true believers.

True Christian worship, whether in a building with other

believers or in your quiet, alone time with God, must be tied to the Word of God and the Spirit of God.

The Word of God is the anchor, and the Spirit of God is the rudder that moves you.

When we read God's Word, nothing new is being told, but new understandings of old truths are being made known to each who reads.

Each of us has different questions and ideas floating around in our heads, but God knows exactly what we need and when we need it.

God's Word speaks to all people, and His goal is to help each of us personally.

Satan will be a problem as long as the earth remains in the state it is. As Christians, seeing where Satan is working is up to us.

I have learned that many people who call themselves Christians don't have a good idea of what it means to follow Christ; and for that Satan is glad. This is why Satan wants and encourages other things in an effort to keep you ignorant.

The first thing you can do for your walk is read daily the Bible to counteract this ignorance. Every day you will find a new understanding and even in eternity we will continue to learn.

The Word has so much depth that it will take all eternity to know everything but in the meantime we will draw strength, peace, and love for God and *from* God daily. We will also see the goodness of God and be able to not *just* survive but fully engage and thrive in our walk with God. We are here to do so much more than we currently understand but most have no clue as to what that means.

Satan works in all people but gets into the heads; easier; of those who are not close in their walk with *the God of the Bible*. This closeness that I'm talking about is *not* a close following of *a religion* but a close understanding of God's Word.

When we are ignorant Satan engages to deceive, like he did in the garden with Eve. And in religions that are immersed in rules and exclusivity, Satan runs the show. I say this because they have God all wrong in so many areas and therefore evil enters and hurts people deep inside.

God doesn't force or make you feel guilty if you don't follow a certain way, in a certain time, and alienates you if you disobey. God gives guidelines that will produce good fruit but *it's still up to you* to chose. And furthermore God is never far away. God is always right there looking for you to hear Him.

Remember the story of Cain? Cain killed his brother and not just his brother but tried killing *the example* of the type of sacrifice offered; that was acceptable to God.

And by the way in Genesis 4:9-10 we read:

> "Then the LORD said to Cain, "Where is Abel your brother?" He said, "I do not know. Am I my brother's keeper?" And He said, "What have you done? The voice of your brother's blood cries out to Me from the ground." (Genesis 4:9-10; NKJV)

My point is that God was still close in proximity to Cain even though God knew what he had done to his brother. God doesn't leave us but waits and often God sends help to change our minds, to bring about a new start.

Abel's story tells of the significance of the coming of God's Son, Jesus Christ, and teaches us a "heart" sacrifice. The heart is the seat of our power, our actions, and our connectedness. God was teaching early on of the significance of "blood".

The blood sacrifice of God's beloved Son who would give everything to make a *simple* way for us to come home. A simple "yes" to follow Jesus is what we need to *begin* a new path that leads us to heaven.

A heart sacrifice is symbolic of a deeper desire from us. The natural physical heart is full of blood; take a look at it for a moment. The blood flows to every part of our body and gives life and when it no longer does this; life is over for that body.

Salvation is life and the blood is what paid the price; the blood of Jesus Christ.

Abel's sacrifice was a blood sacrifice; and before Christ came, was the necessary offering as you read all through the Old Testament. There is a direct link to the heart, to the blood sacrifice of an innocent lamb and to Jesus' ultimate sacrifice that would no longer require us to sacrifce a lamb.

All through the Word everything is connected and everything fits perfectly. You begin to see this as you remain a student of His Word. This is why it becomes easier to see that "*religion*" is not of God but man's way of reaching God.

To a loving Father; who loves His children more than anything; He waits for us *to chose* life again, when we make decisions that remove "life" and cause "death" to rule.

The sacrifice of Abel would set in motion the same understanding and importance of Christ's shed blood. In other words this was important and serious to understand Abels sacrifice even in those days; and so pertaining to the sin of Cain God could have understandably struck Cain down. But God didn't and Satan's lies from the beginning, accusing God of being unmerciful and only wanting His way; are slander and defamation to the Creator of Everything; The Loving Father of all and our only true reason for living. But that's *not* Our Father's true nature.

But when Cain did this and he realized he was a "dead-man walking" he complained to God. God was right there. God heard him and provided the ability to continue living. God wanted Cain to change the same as God wants us to change. God doesn't kill us but our choices reap consequences and shorten our lives.

Before God intervenes He always warns ahead of time so that we will have opportunity to change our ways. God's desire is not to "smite" you, take you down, punish you and send you to a hopeless, horrible place. God's desire is to get you to change your mind. YOUR MIND. Cain was given protection by God after he sinned. Anyone who tried to kill Cain; God gave him a pledge that vengeance would be taken *sevenfold* on anyone who became his murderer. Not an eye for an eye but sevenfold.

And remember after Adam and Eve sinned and realized there nakedness? It says in **Genesis 3:21** that *the LORD God made* tunics of skin, and clothed them. God knew what they had done and it was serious. Because of their actions the whole human race would suffer but God still helped them in their choices. God still loved them as His children. God covered them with skins of an animal that was slain. God gave them something that would remind them at a later time or throughout their lives that life comes from the shedding of blood.

It's always been about the Blood. Life blood flows through us and shedding of blood provides covering and new beginnings. God is Awesome, and GOOD ALL THE TIME! But for many this is not how we see Him.

Religion teaches that God is an angry, judgmental Father ready to smite you if you don't follow a strict set of rules. This began with Satan getting Eve to see God differently. But God has always given us the choice to live as we chose. You might say; yes but if we don't we will go to hell. True that there had to be a place to put Satan and his demons because all that God is; He won't live around the evil. If you want to be with God then you must chose the place where He will be. God didn't create a hell type of place for mankind...remember that. But the rules to follow by in all religions; have been enhanced, made-up, and expounded on; so that we feel such a restriction in just trying to live, that we don't want to be with God.

This is why many don't like Christianity. They have been told such propaganda about God and His ways and the kind of love He is, that nobody really knows God. God wants to love us and He loves us far more than the greatest love story you have ever been told of pure agape love. God wants to give us so many things but we first must chose Him.

Satan loves to hurt us and he appears as an angel of light, as a good and honest only true way; but Jesus is the one you must follow and the Bible is all we need to figure out what our lives should pattern after.

So, the best thing each of us can do is make a place for our personal growth in the Word of God.

Remember to love one another, and when you want to judge, think about how you might have done wrong things before.

We shouldn't judge others by their religion or how they live. We don't know what they are going through or what is in their hearts. But God does know, and there is a power that we can unleash that can change lives in ways far beyond our own understanding.

We need to pray to God to help them and to bless them. Blessing others means asking God to bring them His goodness and love that goes beyond anything Satan or the world can ever do to us.

Satan will be where he wants to be, even in a church. But Satan lives where God does not live. So, the focus is not on Satan but on being everything God wants you to be. And the only way you will know what that is, is to read His Word.

The greatest and most important work of Satan among men and women now is to counterfeit doctrines and experiences of God as revealed in the Scriptures in order to deceive the saints.

In **Ephesians 6:10-18** we see specific instructions about the spiritual warfare of believers.

In **Ephesians 6:10-11** we read;

> "Finally, my brethren, be strong in the Lord and in the power of His might. Put on the whole armor of God, that you may be able to stand against the wiles of the devil." (Ephesians 6:10-11; NKJV)

Here Paul brings serious attention to us. He is saying that having laid before you your high calling and the great doctrines of the gospel, I will now show you the enemies that will oppose you and how you can overcome them.

In the **10th vs.**, the Greek word *endunamoo* is translated as "strong," and it means to *acquire strength* (**Romans 4:20; Philippians 4:13; 2 Timothy 4:17**); *enable* (**1 Timothy 1:12**); *be strong* (**Ephesians 6:10; 2 Timothy 2:1; Hebrews 11:34**); and *increase in strength* (**Acts 9:22**).

In the **11th verse,** the Greek word *panoplia* is translated as "armor," which means to have the full armor of a heavily armed soldier as described in **Ephesians 6:13-17.**

> "Therefore take up the whole armor of God, that you may be able to withstand in the evil day, and having done all, to stand. Stand therefore, having girded your waist with truth, having put on the breastplate of righteousness, and having shod your feet with the preparation of

> the gospel of peace; above all, taking the shield of faith with which you will be able to quench all the fiery darts of the wicked one. And take the helmet of salvation, and the sword of the Spirit, which is the word of God; " (Ephesians 6:13-17; NKJV)

God is revealing how to fight the enemy. This is because we are not to be victims but victorious and we are to remain standing, ready to do battle.

In **Luke 11:22,** we read;

> "But when a stronger than he comes upon him and overcomes him, he takes from him all his armor in which he trusted, and divides his spoils." (Luke 11:22; NKJV)

The armor is very important in order to stand up and resist the enemy.

The "wiles" of the devil are from the Greek word *methodeias*, which means *methods—the different means, plans, and schemes used to deceive, entrap, enslave, and ruin the souls of men.*

Keep in mind Satan doesn't give up. His goal is to destroy your relationship and your walk with God; if one thing doesn't work, he will use another alternative. This is why the armor is so important. Satan is behind much of the troubles that exist in all our personal relationships with one another.

It's not a physical, visible armor as you might think, but it is invisible, and each part is important.

The believer's foes are serious, and they dwell anywhere they can. In **Ephesians 6:12**, we read:

> **"For we do not wrestle against flesh and blood, but against principalities, against powers, against the rulers of the darkness of this age, against spiritual hosts of wickedness in the heavenly places." (Ephesians 6:12; NKJV)**

The war Satan has on all of us is an *epic war*. And what better way for him to hurt us than in the church or place we worship?

Men are commanded to prove and test all doctrines and experiences in the supernatural realm to see if they are of God or of Satan. **(1 Corinthians 2:12-16; Philippians 1:9-10; 1 Thessalonians 5:21-22; 1 John 4:1-6).**

It is certain that every religion, doctrine, and experience among men *cannot* be of God. Therefore, we must judge them by God's plain written Word.

The *knowledge of truth* is the first essential in warfare against demons and error. Great is the danger when believers accept anything and everything in the realm of the supernatural as being from the Lord.

The fact that the believer is a child of God does not stop the devil from trying in every conceivable way *to imitate God to him*. Believers are the ones Satan concentrates on and wars against.

Satan is without principle in taking advantage of men in their weak moments **(Matthew 4:1-11; Luke 22:40; 2 Corinthians 2:11; 11:3)** in tempting men after great success **(John 6:15)**; in suggesting the use of right things in a wrong way and at a wrong time **(Matthew 4:1-11)**; in slandering God to man and man to God **(Genesis 3:1-10; Job 1:6-12; 2:1-7)**; in appearing as an angel of light to deceive **(2 Corinthians 11:14)**; and in deluding his followers as to their eternal end **(2 Thessalonians 2:8-12; Revelations 12:9; 20:7-10)**.

Satan has never been known to be merciful, good, loving, kind, gentle, pitiful, patient, or to have any of the graces of God since he became the enemy of God and man.

In Scripture, he is compared to a *fowler* **(Psalm 91:3)**; a *bird*

(**Matthew 13:4, 19**); a *wolf* (**John 10:12**); a *destroyer* (**John 10:10**); a *roaring lion* (**1 Peter 5:8-9**); a *serpent* (**Revelations 12:9; 20:3**); and a *dragon* (**Revelations 12:3-12**).

Satan goes into the churches and deceives easier because he *appears* good, loving, and looks after your interests.

There are definite ways outlined in Scripture whereby one can detect what kind of spirit is seeking to control him. But if one neglects to study the Word, he may fall prey to one of Satan's demons *through ignorance.*

It must be realized that ignorance is no guarantee against the workings of evil spirits. One of the chief means by which Satan and his forces try to control men ***is through ignorance.***

This accounts for their widespread success in getting men to accept their *suggestions*, *doctrines*, *ideas*, *leadings*, and *guidance*. Among the guiding principles useful in detecting good and evil spirits, and their operations and doctrines, the outstanding ones are these:

- Any doctrine that denies or causes doubt and unbelief concerning anything taught in Scripture is from Satan and his demons (**1 Timothy 4:1-8**). Any religion denying the inspiration of the Bible, the reality of God as a person; the virgin birth, and divinity of Christ, His miraculous power and supernatural ministry; the death, burial, bodily resurrection, and bodily manifestation of Christ after His resurrection; the bodily ascension to heaven and coming again of Jesus Christ to set up a kingdom in the world forever; the necessity of the New Birth, cleansing from sin and living free from sin; and the numerous other experiences of the Bible.

Any religion denying these *fundamental truths* is yielding to "the spirit of error" and not "the spirit of truth" **(1 John 4:1-6).**

- Any power, influence, or doctrine that causes one to become passive, inactive, submissive, and unresisting to the workings of supernatural spirits seeking to control his life contrary to the teachings of Scripture is not of God.

The Bible says, "Resist the devil" **(James 4:7; 1 Peter 5:8-9).** An inclination to approve sin and ignore the necessity of repentance and holy living, and a tendency to remove the penalty for sin or doubt that hell is literal and eternal is promoted by Satan, not God.

Just as God requires truth in the mind for the true working of the Holy Spirit in life, *the devil requires believing lies in men's minds to hold them in bondage.* **(1 Corinthians 6:9-11; 10:12-13; 2 Corinthians 11:3-15; Galatians 5:19-21; 6:7-8; Ephesians 6:10-18; 1 Timothy 4:1-9; James 1:22; 2:10).**

- The Holy Spirit can be recognized by the fruit of the Spirit: love, joy, peace, longsuffering, gentleness, goodness, faith, meekness, and temperance **(Galatians 5:22-23).**

It's important to note the earmarks of Holy Spirit manifestation. A Christ-like spirit of love, patience, and faith in God, soberness and keenness of spirit vision, and deep humility of heart and meekness of spirit, with lion-like courage against sin, sickness, poverty, disease, discouragement, failure, and everything else causing defeat in the Christian life.

There is also absolute clearness of the mental faculties and intelligent action in carrying out Bible instructions concerning known duty and personal life as a Christian.

Holy Spirit manifests in you; freedom from faultfinding, surmising, whispering, and slander; and freedom from all the works of the flesh listed in **Mark 7:19-21; Romans 1:24-32; 1 Corinthians 6:9-11; Galatians 5:19-21; Colossians 3:5-10.**

There is also freedom from any ignorance concerning the divine will. When one is moved upon to act quickly and urgently without knowing whether the act will glorify God, it is better to wait and pray until it is clear that God approves such action.

Remember that **1 John 4:1** commands us to "try the spirits whether they are of God."

Satan is the enemy of all good and the accuser of *God and man* **(Ezekiel 28:11-17; Matthew 13:28; Revelations 12:9-12).**

He is the father of lies and a murderer, as we read in **John 8:44.**

Satan destroys churches. He urges them and their leaders to make religion a paying proposition by appealing to the rich and influential by lowering the standards of holy living, making salvation easy for all, and compromising the essentials of the faith. He does this by feeding the sheep messages on current events in various ways instead of the infallible Word of God.

It is our privilege to stand firmly in the Word of God. Wherever your walk is today, read the Word of God daily, so you will know more about everything in your walk with God. Be proactive in preparing yourself in how to trust God more and stay away from the enemy.

10

"When Satan Goes To Church" Study

FURTHER STUDY

6 Duties of Christians

1. Love your enemies (Matthew 5:43-48)

This is a command. Fill in the blanks for **Matthew 5:44, NKJV**;

> "But I say to you, love your _____, bless those who _____, do good to those who _____, and pray for those who

> _____use you and _____ you."
> (Matthew 5:44; NKJV)

There is power in the Blood of Jesus. When you accept Jesus as Lord and Savior and only follow Him, you will have the power to change and love as Christ did.

2. Strengthen one another

> "But I have prayed for you, that your faith should not fail; and when you have *returned* to Me, strengthen your brethren." (Luke 22:32; NKJV)

The KJV of this verse has "converted" here where the NKJV interprets it as "returned." This does not mean that Peter had not been converted, for he had been and had served God for over 3 years.

It simply refers to the fact that he was headed for a fall, and that he would come back to God and be reconverted becoming stronger than before.

In **Luke 22:32**, NKJV, what did Jesus do for Peter?

After Peter experienced the testing and the prayers of Jesus, what did Jesus ask him to do?

And why is this so important for us to do for one another?

Jesus said that what I do, my Father does. To know the Father and His heart, we simply must look at what Jesus did and know that Our Father is everything the Son is. How has the Father had compassion on you in your life?

3. Do not be ignorant

> "Moreover, brethren, I do not want you to be unaware that all our fathers were under the cloud, all passed through the sea, all were baptized into Moses in the cloud and in the sea, all ate the same spiritual food, and all drank the same spiritual drink. For they drank of that spiritual Rock that followed them, and that Rock was Christ. But with most of them God was not well pleased, for their bodies were scattered in the wilderness." (1 Corinthians 10:1-5; NKJV)

In **1 Corinthians 10:1-5,** we read a serious statement from Paul to the Christians. It seemed that many Corinthians thought that they were secure in their salvation because they had repented, were baptized, and had partaken of Christian ordinances.

According to them, nothing they did could cut them off from Christ – they could still take part in idolatrous feasts and be saved, or so they wanted to believe. **(1 Corinthians 8:4-13; 10:16-33).** This is why Paul made the plain statement in **1 Corinthians 9:27:**

> "But I discipline my body and bring it into subjection, lest, when I have preached to others, I myself should become disqualified." (1 Corinthians 9:27; NKJV)

What did Paul want them to be aware of? **(1 Corinthians 10:1)**

_____

_____

And why do you think the ignorance of the journey before that was passed down from generation to generation was important now?

_____

_____

Accepting Jesus as Lord and Savior is more than a ticket to heaven; it's about what your heart wants.

Don't take it lightly.

Change what you need and learn everything about God daily.

Why does God not want us to be ignorant? And what can you do to change things in your life?

_____

_____

_____

God's WORD Sets You Free

Fill in the blanks:

> "Now concerning _____, brethren, I do not want you to be _____: You know that you were Gentiles, carried away to these dumb _____, however you were led. Therefore I make known to you that no one speaking by the Spirit of God calls Jesus _____, and no one can say that Jesus is Lord except by the _____" (1 Corinthians 12:1-3; NKJV)

> "But I do not want you to be _____, brethren, concerning those who have fallen _____, lest you sorrow as others who have no _____." (1 Thessalonians 4:13; NKJV)

In **1 Thessalonians 5:6-8,** we read how Christians should live. Explain what we should and should not do and why it's important.

_____

_____

What should we put on that God has given us?

_____
_____
_____
_____

4. Stand fast in sound doctrine

> "Therefore, brethren, stand fast and hold the traditions which you were taught, whether by word or our epistle." (2 Thessalonians 2:15; NKJV)

In **2 Thessalonians 2:15,** what two commands are given to Christians?

_____
_____

> "Remind them of these things, charging them before

> the Lord not to strive about words to no profit, to the ruin of the hearers." (2 Timothy 2:14; NKJV)

In **2 Timothy 2:14**, we read about *'Disapproved and Approved Workers.'* In **verse 14** (NKJV), we see the statement "to the ruin of the hearers." The Greek word used is *katastrophe*.

Paul is trying to explain how serious a worker is in teaching *wrong things* or *wrong understandings* of what God meant as vital.

It means to overthrow the faith of men and cause their backsliding when workers teach things not in the Bible as God emphasizes as important or necessary; or do not teach the significance of Salvation and accepting the Blood of Jesus as the only way to heaven. It's serious.

Have you experienced any religious teachings that have caused you great heartache and now know they are not biblical? Or have you never understood that to be saved, you must accept Jesus and Jesus alone as Savior...not a religion or church acceptance will work? Explain.

_____
_____
_____
_____
_____

In **verse 15**, we learn that a true worker gives the true meaning and the true application specifically written in the Word of God. There is no other source to find what God wants.

The chief fundamental principle of interpretation is to gather from the Scriptures themselves the precise meaning the writers intended to convey. With this in mind; we read **2 Timothy 2:15**;

> "Be diligent to present yourself approved to_____, a worker who does not need to be_____, rightly _____ the word of truth." (2 Timothy 2:15; NKJV)

With many opinions, where will you go to get the final answer? Is it only found in "one place" in the Bible, or do you need to sometimes study throughout the Bible to know more in order to come to the correct conclusion? Explain.

_____
_____
_____
_____
_____

Don't take someone's word for it....it might take you down the wrong road and lead you away from your relationship with God.

> "But you must continue in the things which you have learned and been assured of, knowing from whom you have learned them, and that from childhood you have known the Holy Scriptures, which are able to make you wise for salvation through faith which is in Christ Jesus, All Scripture is given by inspiration of God, and is profitable for doctrine, for reproof, for correction, for instruction in righteousness, that the man of God may be complete, thoroughly equipped for every good work." (2 Timothy 3:14-17; NKJV)

In **2 Timothy 3:14-17**, we find a power statement and assurance of the one and only way to understand the Scriptures.

What must we continue in? What will the Holy Scriptures most assuredly do for you?

_____
_____
_____
_____
_____

(2 Timothy 3:14-15; NKJV)

All Scripture is given by what? And is profitable for doctrine (teaching), for reproof (evidence), for correction (to restore), for instruction (schooling) in what?

_____
_____
_____

(2 Timothy 3:16; NKJV)

All this is so the men or women of God may be what? And thoroughly what?

_____
_____
_____
_____

(2 Timothy 3:17; NKJV)

5. *Do not grow weary in doing good*

"But as for you, brethren, do not grow weary in doing

> good. And if anyone does not obey our word in this epistle, note that person and do not keep company with him, that he may be ashamed. Yet do not count him as an enemy, but admonish him as a brother." (2 Thessalonians 3:13-15; NKJV)

In **2 Thessalonians 3:13-15**, Paul says while you refuse to support those who are busybodies and lazy, do not forget the worthy poor. This is the second time this is found in Paul's writing (v 13; Galatians 6:9).

Paul was explaining that some might not agree with the Word, but we were to count them more an *enemy to themselves* than to those who kept true to the Word.

Paul says to admonish him even though you have no common ground in the Word *right now,* for his soul is still of infinite value to God. Paul doesn't encourage you to be mean or shun them.

Have you ever dealt with a similar situation, and if you have, how did you handle it?

6. Be swift to hear, slow to speak, slow to wrath

> "So then, my beloved brethren, let every man be swift to hear, slow to speak, slow to wrath; for the wrath of man does not produce the righteousness of God." (James 1:19-20; NKJV)

In **James 1:19-20** we learn the importance of these words. Why do you think God wants us to exercise self-control over these matters?

These are qualities we need to have during trials. Have you ever experienced the negative when you weren't able to keep yourself from doing these things? Explain how you understood its importance.

_____

_____

7 Things the Word of God is Able To Do (2 Timothy 3:15)

1. Make wise for salvation (v 15; Romans 1:16; James 1:21).

What is the Gospel of Christ as is written in **Romans 1:16**?

_____

2. Produce faith (v 15; Romans 10:17).

What does **Romans 10:17** say where faith comes from?

_____

3. Make Jesus Christ known (v 15; John 5:39; 1 Corinthians 15:1-8).

In **John 5:39** where is it that Jesus says we have eternal life?

_____

4. Build up (Acts 20:32).

Fill in the blank:

> "...I commend you to _____ and to the _____ of His _____, which is able to _____ you _____ and give you an _____ among all those who are _____."
> (Acts 20:32; NKJV)

5. Give inheritance (Acts 20:32).

6. Produce profit in doctrine, reproof, correction, and instruction in righteousness (v 16).

In **2 Timothy 3:16** where is all scripture given by?

_____

7. Make the man of God complete (v 17).

In **2 Timothy 3:17** when the man of God is complete what is he thoroughly equipped for?

_____

26 Branches of Satan's Work

In general the work of Satan is to oppose God whenever possible. For this reason his work varies in some respects with the purposes of God in different ages and dispensations. In the Old Testament times Satan's great work was to cause the fall of man, seize his dominion, and try to prevent the coming of the Messiah into the world in order to avert his own defeat and pending doom.

We see in **Genesis 6:1-4** how Satan caused fornication from the fallen angels to do away with pure Adamite stock. The giants were the results. This was the effort to ruin the pure line where Jesus would come forth.

> "Now it came to pass, when men began to multiply on the face of the earth, and daughters were born to them, that the sons of God saw the daughters of men, that they were beautiful; and they took wives for themselves of all whom they chose. And the LORD said, "My Spirit shall not strive with man forever, for he is indeed flesh; yet his days shall be one hundred and twenty years. There were giants on the earth in those days, and also afterward, when the sons of God came in to the daughters of men and they bore children to them. Those were the mighty men who were of old, men of renown." (Genesis 6:1-4; NKJV)

God gave Adam 810 years before and 120 more years as stated in **v 3**. This was God's mercy. He reminded Adam that things had changed since the fall and that Adam was now flesh because of his choice to sin, and that he would die. The fact is, **v 3** reveals that Adam had corrupted his way upon earth as all other flesh had done, and that God, in His mercy, gave him 120 more years in which to repent and conform his life to the will of his creator. Whether Adam did this or not is not known.

It says in **v 2** and **v 4** we see "sons of God" and "daughters of men"; but who are they? What are your thoughts?

The "sons of God" are the product of God. Seth did not have a son until 235 years after creation, and his son did not have a son until 325 years after creation **(Genesis 5:3, 6, 9)**. Where did these sons come from? They could not have been sons of Seth, for these marriages took place when men began to multiply -- in the very beginning of the race before Seth had sons of marriageable age. The terms "sons of God" proves that they were the product of God, not of Seth. They were fallen angels of **1 Peter 3:19; 2 Peter 2:4; Jude 6-7**.

Also it's good to understand **v 4** in that the "sons of God" married the "daughters of men", as before the flood, giants were again born to them. This defintely answers the question of where the giants before and after the flood came from **(Genesis 6:1-4)**.

To further understand what it means when referring to the

"daughters of men" we need to look at the Hebrew word used in **v 2**. The Hebrew word for "men," is adam, and is in the singular, specifically signifying the man Adam and not the daughers of Cain, Seth, or men in general. Then in **v 4** we see the same statement, "daughters of men". It was not the daughters of Cain as supposed, for no daughters of Cain could be on this side of the flood. They were all killed by the flood **(Genesis 6:18; 7:7; 8:18; 9:1; 1 Peter 3:20)**. Women bore/had children by fallen, wicked angels as well as by men. It was not necessary to emphasize having children by men, but having children by angels was something to make special mention of **(v 4; Jude 6-7)**. It was because of this great sin that the Lord was "sorry that He had made man on the earth" **(v 6)**.

Now the mention of "men of renown" **(v 4)**, is very interesting. The Hebrew word for men is *shem*, referring to men of name, honor, and authority **(Numbers 16:2; Ezekiel 16:14-15; 34:29; 39:13; Daniel 9:15)**. The giants became the heroes of Greek mythology and primitive truth now corrupted by misinformation over the years.

It's important to understand that there is so much information in every verse and we want to take our time and learn what everything means.

Now it's time to look at the ***26 Branches of Satan's Work*** among us. We need to be aware of how much Satan interferes in every aspect of our lives. God knows that the struggle to live on earth is largely because of this kind of medling that Satan does in our lives. But furthermore we also need to be proactive and keep Satan out of our business.

1. He is the deciever of all mankind (2 Corinthians 11:14; Revelations 12:9; 20:1-10).

2. He exercised the power of death until Christ conquered death, hell, and the grave (Hebrews 2:14; Revelations 1:18).

3. He is the leader of all sinners and backsliders of the human race (1 John 3:8-10; 1 Timothy 5:15), and all spirit rebels (Matthew 9:34; Ephesians 6:10-18).

4. He causes all sickness, disease, and physical and mental maladies in the human race (Luke 13:16; Acts 10:38).

5. Takes advantage of all adversities of mankind to further their rebellion and hold them captive (2 Corinthians 2:11; 1 Timothy 1:20; 5:11-15).

6. Tempts mankind (Mark 1:13; 1 Corinthians 7:5).

7. Provokes to sin (1 Chronicles 21:1).

8. Causes offense (Matthew 16:23).

9. Transforms himself into an angel of light (2 Corinthians 11:14).

10. Resists others (Zechariah 3:1-2).

11. Enters into union with others against God (Luke 22:3; John 13:2).

12. Sends messengers to defeat saints (2 Corintians 12:7).

13. Hinders the gospel (Acts 13:10; 1 Thessalonians 2:18).

14. Steals the word of God from mankind lest they should believe it (Matthew 13:19; Luke 8:12).

15. Works miracles (2 Thessalonians 2:9).

16. Contends with messengers of God, endeavoring to hold them captive (Daniel 10:12-21; Jude 9).

17. Hinders answers to prayer (Daniel 10:12-21).

18. Sets snares for mankind to fall into sin (1 Timothy 3:7; 2 Timothy 2:26).

19. Causes diversion and blinds men to the gospel (2 Corinthians 4:4).

20. Causes double-mindedness (James 1:5-9).

21. Causes doubt and unbelief (Genesis 3:4-5; Romans 14:23).

22. Causes darkness and oppression (2 Corinthians 4:4; 2 Peter 1:4-9).

23. Causes deadness and weakness (Hebrews 6:1; 9:14).

24. Causes delay and compromise (Acts 24:25; 26:28).

25. Causes division and strife (1 Corinthians 3:1-3; 1 Peter 5:8).

26. Makes war on the saints (Ephesian 6:10-18).

Power of One Voice, LLC
Come Alive Series

11

Be Strong in The Lord

"Finally, my brethren, be strong in the Lord and in the power of His might." (Ephesians 6:10; NKJV)

In the Christian life, we battle against rulers and authorities; powerful evil forces of fallen angels are headed by the devil, a vicious fighter.

After having laid before us our high calling and the great doctrines of the gospel, Paul was explaining, showing us the enemies that will oppose us and how we can overcome them.

The Greek word translated as "strong" is *endunamoo*, which means to acquire strength, in **Ephesians 6:10**.

To explain what this means, we turn to **Romans 4:20**;

> **"He did not waver at the promise of God through unbelief, but was strengthened in faith, giving glory to God," (Romans 4:20; NKJV)**

Abraham never doubted that God would fulfill His promise. Abraham's life was marked by mistakes, sins, and failures, as well as by wisdom and goodness, but he consistently trusted God.

His faith was strengthened by the obstacles he faced, and his life was an example of faith in action. He would have given up in despair if he had looked only at his own resources for subduing Canaan and founding a nation. But Abraham looked to God, obeyed Him, and waited for God to fulfill His Word.

And in **Philippians 4:13,** we read;

> **"I can do all things through Christ who strengthens me." (Philippians 4:13; NKJV)**

Paul could get along happily because he could see life from God's point of view. He focused on what he was supposed to do, not what he felt he should have.

Paul had his priorities straight and was grateful for everything

God had given him. He had detached himself from the non-essentials so that he could concentrate on the eternal.

Often the desire for more or better possessions is a longing to fill an empty place in a person's life. Ask yourself, to what are you drawn when you feel empty inside? How can you find true contentment? The answer lies in your perspective, priorities, and power source.

But in **Philippians 4:13**, is it saying we can do everything we desire? The power we receive in union with Christ is sufficient to do His will and face the challenges arising from our commitment to doing it.

He does not grant us the superhuman ability to accomplish anything we can imagine without regard to His interest. We will face troubles, pressures, and trials as we contend for faith. As they come, ask Christ to strengthen you.

In **2 Timothy 4:17-18**, we see that the Lord is faithful in all things and stays with you all thru the difficulties.

> "But the Lord stood with me and strengthened me, so that the message might be preached fully through me, and that all the Gentiles might hear. Also, I was delivered out of the mouth of the lion. And the Lord will deliver me from every evil work and preserve me

> for His heavenly kingdom. To Him be glory forever and ever. Amen!" (2 Timothy 4:17-18; NKJV)

Timothy was probably not feeling very brave with his mentor in prison and his church in turmoil. Paul may have been subtly telling Timothy that the Lord had called him to preach and would give him the courage to continue.

God always gives us the strength to do what He has commanded. However, this strength may not be evident until we step out in faith and begin doing the task.

When no man stood with Paul, the Lord did. He, the Lord, delivered Paul from this particular trouble and blessed his ministry among the Gentiles.

His statement of being delivered out of the mouth of the lion may have been an expression denoting deliverance from imminent danger.

We need to be ready every moment to resist the devil. Our enemies are associated with Satan.

Satan is the **ultimate bad guy,** and he has enlisted many to fight and *confuse* the world. Confusion is his master play. Satan never ceases to be hostile toward us; he is constantly accusing us before God.

Look at **Zechariah 3:1-2**:

> "Then he showed me Joshua the high priest standing before the Angel of the LORD, and Satan standing at his right hand to oppose him. And the LORD said to Satan, "The LORD rebuke you, Satan! The LORD who has chosen Jerusalem rebuke you! Is this not a brand plucked from the fire!" (Zechariah 3:1-2; NKJV)

This is not referring to Joshua, who led Israel in the conquest of Canaan. In some translations, this scripture has his name spelled *Jeshua*. He was Israel's high priest when the remnant returned to Jerusalem and began rebuilding the walls **(Haggai 1:1, 12; 2:4)**.

Zechariah saw him standing before (in the presence of) the Angel of the LORD and Satan standing by to resist him. The LORD rebuked Satan and refused to let him stop the restoration of Judah and Jerusalem. Twice Satan was rebuked **(v 1-2)**.

Satan accused Jeshua, who here represents the nation of Israel. The accusations were accurate – Jeshua stood in "filthy" clothes (sins). Yet God revealed his mercy, stating that he chose to save his people in spite of their sins.

Satan is always accusing people of their sins before God (Job 1:6). But he greatly *misunderstands* the breadth of God's mercy and forgiveness toward those who believe in him.

In **Deuteronomy 31:6-8** we see that God wanted Israel and Joshua to be strong and of good courage, never fearing because ***God was with them***. This is the Joshua many of us are more familiar with.

> "Be strong and of good courage, do not fear nor be afraid of them; for the LORD your God, He is the One who goes with you. He will not leave you nor forsake you. Then Moses called Joshua and said to him in the sight of all Israel, "Be strong and of good courage, for you must go with this people to the land which the LORD has sworn to their fathers to give them, and you shall cause them to inherit it. And the LORD, He is the One who goes before you. He will be with you, He will not leave you nor forsake you; do not fear nor be dismayed." (Deuteronomy 31:6-8; NKJV)

There are three commands here. The first ***one is to Israel***; be strong and of good courage, do not fear nor be afraid of them. The second ***one is to Joshua***; be strong and of good courage. And the *third **one is to all***; do not fear nor be dismayed.

This counsel to Joshua and Israel can also be for us today. Faith brings incredible blessings, and God wants us to trust Him for everything. He wants us to do this with courage.

In order to accomplish this, we must pray and *know that God will deliver* and wait for His "time." We must not waver but simply *tell God we trust Him.*

Work as if the end result is already done. This is how to be strong in the Lord.

In **Deuteronomy 31:22-23** we see that Moses wrote a song giving charge to Joshua. God has a song written to remind the children of Israel that He is always the same and encourages them as they sing it over and over.

> "Therefore, Moses wrote this song the same day and taught it to the children of Israel. Then He inaugurated Joshua the son of Nun, and said, 'Be strong and of good courage; for you shall bring the children of Israel into the land of which I swore to them, and I will be with you.'" (Deuteronomy 31:22-23; NKJV)

This is not only a request but a command. Like many commands, God wants us to do them because *they are the power of life and death.*

God had Moses write a song so it would be a reminder.

When we obey the commands of God, we will find greater growth in our walk. God is not trying to force you to do anything, but when you see the seriousness of life and death and know the heart of God wants you home with Him for all eternity, you understand why certain things are commanded.

Be strong and of good courage; do not fear or doubt that God will help you.

All of this works perfectly together to formulate the end result; a greater faith and trust in God.

For your benefit, a loving Father, Our Father in Heaven, commands that we do these things to see how much it helps our faith grow.

When we have more faith, which God wants us to have, we can take authority over our lives and our world in bringing more of God's grace and purpose to earth.

In **1 Chronicles 22:13**, we read;

> "Then you will prosper, if you take care to fulfill the statutes and judgments with which the LORD charged Moses concerning Israel. Be strong and of good cour-

> **age; do not fear nor be dismayed." (1 Chronicles 22:13; NKJV)**

This is the basis of prosperity in any realm—obeying God to the letter. **(Joshua 1:1-8)**

God expresses the need to obey Him so that our hearts can grow in understanding, knowing that all things work together for those who love the Lord.

Many people know what's right and do what's right for *certain people, leaving* others who long for their friendship or love out in the cold.

God always deals with the *heart.* When we obey God, we also trust that God's desire to obey Him is in our best interest.

God is not impressed if you are divided, remaining hurtful to some you have not forgiven while being extra good to those it's easy to do for. God wants a clean and sincere heart; it only comes when you walk with Him.

In **Psalm 1:3,** we see four *blessings of the righteous.*

> **"They are like trees planted along the riverbank,**

> **bearing fruit each season. Their leaves never wither, and they prosper in all they do." (Psalm 1:3; NKJV)**

The phrase "they prosper in all they do" does not mean immunity to failure or difficulties. Nor does it guarantee health, wealth, and happiness. What the Bible means by prosperity is this: When we apply God's wisdom, the fruit (results or by-products) we bear will be good and receive God's approval.

The analogy of a tree soaking up water, thus bearing luscious fruit, we also are to soak up God's Word. This will produce actions and attitudes that honor God. We must have God's Word in our hearts to achieve anything worthwhile.

God is giving you the tools to be strong and fight the good fight. Forgiveness is something that removes the past. Please forgive and leave the past alone. Stop destroying your future!

In **Psalms 1:2**, there are *7 things of a Righteous Person.* These things represent actions we must purposely live daily.

1. **Delights in the Word of God (Psalm 1:2).**
2. **Meditates in it day & night (Psalm 1:2).**
3. **Consecrates himself to obey it (Psalm 1:1).**
4. **Makes it his rule of life and conduct (James 1:22-27).**

5. **Makes it his standard of faith and religion (2 Timothy 3:16-17).**
6. **Reads it to gain knowledge and wisdom (Matthew 24:15; Ephesians 3:4; Revelations 1:3).**
7. **Feeds on it to grow spiritually (1 Peter 2:1-3; Romans 10:17).**

Your relationship with God makes you strong in the Lord and not "religion." Please focus on what God says in His Word, first and foremost.

In **1 Samuel 4:7-11,** the prophecy of **1 Samuel 2:34** is fulfilled. Israel is defeated: thirty thousand were slain, and the ark is captured. What's interesting in this story is the switch from Israel being the victor to the Philistines being the victor.

The Philistines were afraid because they remembered stories about God's intervention for Israel when they left Egypt. But Israel had turned away from God and was now clinging to only *a form of godliness*, symbolizing former victories.

Today, people and/or churches often try to live on the memories of God's blessings. The Israelites wrongly assumed that because God had given them victory in the past, he would do it again, even though they had strayed far from him.

Today, as in Bible times, spiritual victories come through a continually renewed relationship with God.

Don't live off the past. Keep your relationship with God new and fresh every day.

The Israelites rightly recognized the great holiness of the Ark, but they thought that the Ark itself—the wood and metal box—was their source of power. They began to use it *as a good luck charm*, expecting it to protect them from their enemies.

A symbol of God does not guarantee His presence and power. Their attitude toward the Ark came perilously close to idol worship. Keep in mind that if "going" to a church gathering is your justification for spending time with God on a weekly basis, this is very similar to what we just talked about.

Having God's presence in your daily life can save you from making wrong decisions that hurt you.

Becoming proactive in spending daily time with God will give you the power and understanding of what you need to do in your daily life.

If you don't put gas in your vehicle, it will eventually have no power, and the same goes for the fuel you feed your heart and soul.

When the Ark was captured by their enemies, they thought that Israel's glory was gone **(1 Samuel 4:19-22)** and that God had deserted them **(1 Samuel 7:1-2)**.

God uses His power according to His own wisdom and will. He responds to *the faith* of those who seek Him.

In **1 Samuel 4:19-22**, the incident illustrates Israel's spiritual darkness and decline. This young boy, Ichabod, was supposed to succeed his father, Phinehas, in the priesthood, but his father had been killed because he was an evil man who desecrated the Tabernacle. The terror of God leaving his people overshadowed the joy of childbirth.

When sin dominates our lives, even God-given joys and pleasures seem empty.

Being strong in the Lord is something "we must *choose*." In **1 Samuel 7,** Israel mourned, and sorrow gripped the nation for 20 years because the Ark was captured.

The Ark was put away like an unwanted box in an attic, and it seemed as if the Lord had abandoned His people.

Samuel, now a grown man, roused them to action by saying that if they were truly sorry, they should do something about it.

How easy it is for us to complain about our problems, even to God, while we refuse to act, change, and do what He requires.

Before you blame God for your problems, ask yourself if

there is something He has already told you to do and you have neglected it.

You may not receive new guidance from God until you have acted on His previous directions. God is teaching you, but you must be ready to come up higher.

In **1 Chronicles 28:10,** we read;

> "Consider now, for the LORD has chosen you to build a house for the sanctuary, be strong, and do it. (1 Chronicles 28:10; NKJV)

This is a warning to Solomon, who became God's son (**1 Chronicles 28:6**), and applies to all sons of God: they must not forsake Him **(v 9-10)**. God chose Solomon. Solomon did not choose God first.

So, it is with all men. God chose to redeem man. Man did not choose to have God redeem him. In other words, God made His plan known to man and required that every individual choose Him or Satan.

In **John 3:16,** we read that God is the one who gave long before the man gave to Him;

> "For God so loved the world that He gave His only begotten Son, that whoever believes in Him should not perish but have everlasting life." (John 3:16; NKJV)

In **John 15:16,** God chose you and not the other way around.

> "You did not choose Me, but I chose you and appointed you that you should go and bear fruit, and that your fruit should remain, that whatever you ask the Father in My name He may give you." (John 15:16; NKJV)

You are chosen by God and ordained to go and bear fruit, produce eternal works, and get an answer to every prayer. God gives us eternal life and the ability to work with Him and so much more.

In the prior verse, **John 15:15,** Jesus says I am not going to make you bond slaves. I make you full partners and My personal representatives on earth. You are to represent Me and reproduce My works as I represented God and did His works. You will share equally with Me in My inheritance if you share in sufferings and work. You are to share with Me all the things the Father has made known.

> "I no longer call you slaves, because a master doesn't confide in his slaves. Now you are my friends, since I have told you everything the Father told me." (John 15:15; NLT)

Because Jesus Christ is Lord and Master, He should call us servants; instead, He calls us friends. How comforting and reassuring to be chosen as Christ's friend! Because He is Lord and Master, we owe Him our unqualified obedience, but most of all, Jesus asks us to obey Him because we love Him.

Remember that Jesus made the first choice – to live and die for us, to invite us to live with Him forever. We make the next choice–to accept or reject His offer. Without His choice, we would have no choice to make.

God's mercy is greater than we even understand.

In **2 Peter 3:9,** we read:

> "The Lord is not slack concerning His promise, as some count slackness, but is longsuffering toward us, not willing that any should perish but that all should come to repentance." (2 Peter 3:9; NKJV)

This shows us why God has *delayed so long* in putting down all rebellion and tolerating His enemies to continue their evil designs.

For years I have felt that "religion" divides, yet I realize now that God is often misrepresented through even the sincerest religions.

Today we need to get to know God on a personal level, and the only way to do that is to read His Word. And furthermore, this requires a personal relationship through the efforts we put forth on a daily basis.

Keep in mind that *no religion* can do this for you. Some religions thrive on the belief that theirs is the 'only way.' This traps them into believing they are better than others (self-righteousness or self-exaltation), and they are immune to many things (trusting in their religion) they might otherwise need to address in their walk with God. It's entrapment.

God wants us to grow, so stay away from man-made ideas that take you down wrong, winding roads.

If you know the Word, you will know the ministry Jesus brought. But to know what the Bible says takes study and not just a single verse. Know the context and the complete message of God on subjects.

Jesus didn't come to start another religion but only to

confirm that our *relationship* is exclusively the way to knowing the Father. Work on your relationship by reading and praying daily, and if you find a church that teaches the Bible as God's truth, you will grow even more.

In **Revelations 22:17,** we read a powerful proclamation of how God continues to feel about all men, *not just a few.*

This is an invitation to *all men* to be saved.

> "And the Spirit and the bride say, "Come!" And let him who hears say, "Come!" And let him who thirsts come. Whoever desires, let him take the water of life freely." (Revelations 22:17; NKJV)

There are three classes of people invited. Those who hear, those who are thirsty, and those who will come. Thus, all men are invited to *freely partake in the water of life.*

Man is a free moral agent. If man were not a free moral agent, God would be entirely responsible for all sin, the effects of sin, rebellion, sickness, and the damnation of men, demons, and angels.

In expressing the need for us to be strong in the Lord,

we must understand that God created us as free moral agents, meaning we can and will make choices.

Thus, it is and always will be *our choice to be* strong in the Lord.

In understanding what it means to have a free moral responsibility, we need to see the reality of who we are and our journey to earth.

Take some time and look at these points in reference to **Man Being a Free Moral Agent**.

Study the Scripture:

1. Man has no choice about coming into the world, but after he is here and old enough to be responsible, he is held *accountable* **for his salvation or damnation (Mark 16:15-16; Luke 13:3, 5).**

2. Man has his will to exercise in this matter (John 3:16; 6:37; 7:17; Revelations 22:17).

3. It is God's will that all men who will be shall be saved (Revelations 22:17; John 3:16; 1 Timothy 2:4; 2 Peter 3:9).

4. Men are commanded to choose God (Joshua 24:15; Luke 13:3, 5).

5. Men are to be cursed if they do not choose God (Proverbs 1:29-33; Mark 16:16; Isaiah 66:3).

6. It is impossible to serve God and Satan at the same time (Matthew 6:24; John 8:32-36; Romans 6:16-23; 8:12-13).

7. Promises are given to men upon the basis of their choice (Revelations 22:17; Matthew 16:24-25; Mark 3:35; 16:16; John 3:16; 5:40; 7:17; 9:31; 12:26).

In over 4,000 Scriptures where to *choose, will,* and other words expressing willpower are used, not one suggests that God forces any man to accept Him and do His will. Man's relationship with God is voluntary **(Revelations 22:17; Mark 16:16; John 3:16; 7:17; 1 Peter 5:2).**

No man or woman recognizing that endless decisions are necessary to daily life can deny the fact of free acts and conduct, for he or she knows that they have complete freedom of action —moral action—concerning right and wrong and that they are responsible to God for every act.

If one can deny these facts, one can also deny their very existence and prove it on the same basis that they try to prove that they are not a moral agent. We are each free to choose our own destiny, and daily moral actions are facts known to sane beings.

In **1 Corinthians 16:13-14** Paul writes 5 commands concerning our dedication to Christ.

> "Watch, stand fast in the faith, be brave, be strong. Let all that you do be done with love." (1 Corinthians 16:13-14; NKJV)

When it says to watch, it means to be continually on your guard.

We might be watching for Christ's coming, being careful not to enter into temptation, remembering that we are *worthy* to escape all tribulations, being prayerful and sober, and spending time daily with God.

Standing fast in the faith means keeping rank, not being disorderly or retreating. It's important to keep unity, not be prideful or judgmental, and remember you also have troubles.

Let nothing divide you so Satan cannot defeat you. Be brave, do not flinch in the fight. Maintain your ground at all costs. Resist and press forward.

Be strong, keeping yourself fit. Learn how to conquer. **(Luke 1:80; 2:40; Ephesians 3:16).** And do all things in love **(1 Corinthians 13:4-7)**

The secret to victory over sin is in harmony with God's Word. We read in **1 John 2:14**;

> "I have written to you, fathers, Because you have known Him who is from the beginning. I have written to you, young men, Because you are strong, and the word of God abides in you, And you have overcome the wicked one." (1 John 2:14; NKJV)

I leave with this thought on our Savior's childhood. Jesus, as a young boy, set his heart on the things of God, and so can we.

In **Luke 2:40,** we read;

> "And the Child grew and became strong in spirit, filled with wisdom; and the grace of God was upon Him." (Luke 2:40; NKJV)

Here are 10 Facts about Jesus:

1. **Grew in the body (v 40).**

2. **Grew strong in mind (v 40).**
3. **Was filled with wisdom (v 40).**
4. **Lived in God's grace (v 40).**
5. **Had a gift of teaching (v 47).**
6. **Knew His life mission (v 49).**
7. **Was a model boy (v 51).**
8. **Increased in wisdom (v 52).**
9. **Grew to maturity, adulthood (v 52).**
10. **Grew in favor with God and man (v 52; Psalm 119:97-104; Isaiah 50:4)**

We read in **Isaiah 50:4-5**;

> "The Lord GOD has given Me the tongue of the learned, That I should know how to speak a word in season to him who is weary. He awakens Me morning by morning, He awakens My ear to hear as the learned. The Lord GOD has opened My ear, And I was not rebellious, Nor did I turn away." (Isaiah 50:4-5; NKJV)

These verses refer to the personal training of the Messiah from childhood by God through the Holy Spirit. He no doubt was filled with the Holy Spirit from birth, as John the Baptist was.

He also had human teachers, as we read in **Psalm 119:97-104.** No less than 7 times, the Messiah, while on earth, claimed to speak only what God had given Him to speak **(John 7:16; 8:28, 46, 47; 12:49; 14:10, 24; 17:8).**

In **Psalms 119:97-104**, we understand more fully that the Lord Jesus Christ is our strength because He was the sinless One.

When it comes to being holy and true to God's Word and hating every sin, no man other than Christ can say this has been true of his entire life.

The Messiah outshines all others as far as sinlessness in the entire life is concerned.

Jesus had:

1. Wisdom above all enemies through the commandments was singularly true of Messiah **(v 97-98).**
2. More understanding than teachers through meditation in God's Word, more than any other man. **(v 99; Isaiah 11:1-2; 42:1-5; 50:4-6; 61:1-2; Luke 2:40, 52).**
3. Understanding more than the ancients through keeping the divine precepts was true of Messiah **(v 100; Luke 2:40, 46-52).**
4. Restraining feet from every evil way to obey the Word of God was only true of the Messiah **(v 101; 1 Peter 2:21-22).**

5. Absolute union with God's judgments without the least departure from them was only true of Messiah **(v 102; 1 Peter 2:21-22)**.
6. Complete satisfaction with God's Word was true of Messiah alone **(v 103; Hebrews 10:9)**.
7. Hatred of every false way through intelligent conformity to the Word of God was also true of Messiah only **(v 104; Hebrews 1:9; 1 Peter 2:21-22)**.

It is true that any godly man could be a double fulfillment with the Messiah in some details of v 97-104, but when it comes to being literally holy and true to God's Word and hating every sin, no man other than Christ can say that this has been true of his entire life.

It is true of many after conversion or becoming a new creature in Christ, but the Messiah outshines all others concerning sinlessness in the entire life. **(Hebrews 1:9; 1 Peter 2:21-22)**.

It is clear that Christ and His doctrines are to be a blessing to the Godly and an offense to stumble at; the ungodly.

6 Secrets of Messiah's Sinlessness (Psalms 119:101-104)

1. **Restraining feet from every evil way (v 101).**
2. **Obedience to God's Word.**
3. **Absolute adherence to God's justice and judgments (v 102).**
4. **Instruction from God.**
5. **Love and delight in truth (v 103).**
6. **Hating every false way (v 104).**

In **Isaiah 9:6,** we are reminded that there are **5 names given to clarify Messiah and His purpose.**

Wonderful counselor, mighty God, everlasting Father, and Prince of Peace. These descriptive titles share with us where real strength comes from; for us to have victory in our lives.

In **Psalms 119:105** we read:

> "Your Word is a lamp to my feet and a light to my path." (Psalms 119:105; NKJV)

48 Fold Description of the Word of God (Psalm 119)

1. The law of the Lord (v 1, 18).
2. A record of His testimonies (v 2,14, 31, 36).
3. A revelation of His ways (v 3, 15).
4. A code of His precepts (v 4, 15).
5. A list of His statues (v 5, 33).
6. The sum of His commandments (v 6, 32, 35, 86).
7. The righteous judgements of God (v 7, 13, 62, 75, 106).
8. The source of cleansing (v 9).
9. The words of God (v 11, 16, 57).
10. A ready Counselor (v 24).
11. The source of life (v 25, 40, 50, 88).
12. A history of God's wondrous works (v 27).
13. A tower of strength (v 28).
14. The way of truth (v 30, 142, 151).
15. The way of God (v 1, 37).
16. The way of righteousness (v 40).
17. The way of salvation (v 41).
18. A true trust (v 42).
19. The word of truth (v 43, 142, 151).

20. *The source of hope (v 49, 81, 114).*
21. *A source of comfort (v 52).*
22. *The subject of songs (v 54).*
23. *The foundation of good judgment and knowledge (v 66, 130).*
24. *A source of delight (v 70, 92).*
25. *Something better than riches (v 72).*
26. *A book of promised mercies (v 76).*
27. *The testimony of His mouth (v 88).*
28. *An eternal plan (v 89-91).*
29. *An unforgettable code of laws (v 93).*
30. *Something infinite in its scope (v 96).*
31. *A source of wisdom (v 98).*
32. *A source of knowledge (v 99, 104, 130).*
33. *Something sweeter than honey (v 103).*
34. *A lamp to the feet (v 105).*
35. *A light to the pathway of life (v 105).*
36. *An eternal heritage (v 111).*
37. *A source of joy if obeyed (v 111-112).*
38. *A stay in trouble (v 116).*
39. *Something to be feared (v 120).*
40. *The word of God's righteousness (v 123).*
41. *Something to be loved more than silver and gold (v 127).*

42. **Something wonderful (v 129).**

43. **The source of light (v 130).**

44. **Something understandable to the simple (v 130).**

45. **A code of laws for the upright (v 137).**

46. **A righteous and faithful testimony of God (v 138).**

47. **The pure Word of God (v 140).**

48. **The truth from the beginning (v 160).**

In **Revelations 19:12-13** we read:

> "His eyes were like a flame of fire, and on His head were many crowns. He had a name written that no one knew except Himself. He was clothed with a robe dipped in blood, and His name is called The Word of God. And the armies in heaven, clothed in fine linen, white and clean, followed Hi on white horses." (Revelations 19:12-14; NKJV)

The Word of God is the power of all things from God and of God. It holds the keys to everything in the kingdom.

God's WORD Sets You Free

> "In the beginning was the Word, and the Word was with God, and the Word was God." (John 1:1; NKJV)

The Word refers to Christ and proves His pre-existence. He is the eternal Being as are also the Father and the Holy Spirit. They make the Divine Trinity. Not only was the Word with God, but He was God and always will be as much divine as the other two members of the Trinity **(Psalm 45:6-7; Isaiah 9:6-7; John 1:1; Hebrews 1:8-12; Revelations 1:8, 11; 22:13-16).**

May God help you study and learn scripture daily to know that you are not alone and that God is fighting for you. Learn to follow Him more closely.

12

"Be Strong In The Lord" Study

Further Study

Christianity is a very practical path that God wants us to follow. In **Philippians 4:9**, we read:

> "The things which you learned and received and heard and saw in me, these do, and the God of peace will be with you." (Philippians 4:9; NKJV)

Not only are Christians to meditate on certain things, but also we must *do* certain things. The practicality of Christianity reveals it is not a dead, dry, formal, human religion of rituals, outward

God's WORD Sets You Free

form, and show, but a divine, living, vital, dynamic, liberating way to live. Any religion or path of life; without power to deliver men from sin, sickness, poverty, and want is not of God. **(Matthew 7:7-11; 17:20; 21:22; Mark 9:23; 11:22-24; 16:17-18; John 14:12-15; 15:7, 16; 16:23-26; Hebrews 11; James 1).**

We learn that God encourages us in these things:

4 Things to Practice and Enjoy

1. Things learned - Christian practices

2. Things received - Christian blessings

3. Things heard - Christian blessings

4. Things seen - Christian miracles

Please name 4 things that you have received as blessings, miracles or practices that have been given to you from God:

1. _____

2. _____

3. _____

4. _____

Remember that not only are Christians meditating on certain things, but they are also to do certain things.

Worry

In **Philippians 4:7,** we read:

> "And the peace of God, which surpasses all understanding, will guard your hearts and minds through Christ Jesus." (Philippians 4:7; NKJV)

The Greek word *phroureo* (garrison) means to keep watch or guard. Translated *kept* **(Galatians 3:23; 1 Peter 1:5)**; *guard* **(Philippians 4:7)**, and *guarding with a garrison* **(2 Corinthians 11:32).** When you see the original text and its meaning you take on a newer definition as well as the seriousness for why God wrote this in the first place.

In **Galatians 3:23** it states in the New Living Translation:

> "Before the way of faith in Christ was available to us, we were placed under guard by the law, We were kept in protective custody, so to speak, until the way of faith was revealed." (Galatians 3:23; NLT)

The picture of the law as a guardian is similar to a tutor giving a young child supervision. We no longer need that kind of supervision. The law teaches us *the need for* salvation; God's grace gives us that salvation.

Can the law save us?

_____

Is the guard in **Galatians 3:23** God's protective love for His children?

_____

In **Ephesians 6**, we read how we are to partner with God by engaging in the battles of life and not just sitting on the sideline just coping with the evil as it is dished out to us. God explains the armor He gives us. This is the "power of believers" against the enemy.

There are two kinds of Armor. In **Ephesians 6:13 (NKJV)**, what does it say to take up, and what will you be able to do when you do this?

_____

Name the 6 parts of the Armor as written in **Ephesians 6:**

1. _____

2. _____

3. _____

4. _____

5. _____

6. _____

God's Word clearly states that He is with us in helping us to fight the battles. What can we do to help our relationship with the Father grow stronger and be more and more an open door to strengthen that relationship?

_____

_____

How does this help us when we are told not to worry?

_____

We are in a spiritual battle with a demonic enemy who wants us to fail and to feel hopeless. But God gives us the necessary tools we need, and when we look more closely at scripture and the original words used to describe things, we begin to get a new order of business for our lives.

In **Deuteronomy 3:21-22** what does it say that the LORD our God will do for us in the battle?

_____

Let's not live in defeat but be victorious. God never wanted us to just scrape by or just sit by the wayside and hope all will pass. No, God gave us tools to fight the enemy and to have victory. It's not only for outward victory as in a physical manifestation, but it is even more important to have the victory in our thinking that leads to our actions.

Imagine never worrying about anything! It seems impossible; we all have worries on the job, in our homes, at school, and in many places and situations.

In **Philippians 4:6,** 7, Paul's advice is to turn our worries into prayers. Do you want to worry less? Then pray more, and whenever you start to worry, just give it to God. God has our back, and He sees everything. Voice your trust and faith in God, and tell Him you want His work in your life. This will increase your faith as each situation comes your way. Of course, many decisions have to be made immediately, and knowing what it means to live right will guide you. Here are a few ways to work on "worry."

10 Secrets of Cure for Worry

1. Permit the peace of God to garrison or keep your heart and mind through Christ Jesus.

What are we kept by in **1 Peter 1:5**?

_____

2. Renounce all worry and make all requests known to God by prayer, supplication, and thanksgiving.

In **Philippians 4:6,** How are we to make our requests to God known?

_____
_____
_____

3. Think about the right things.

In **Philippians 4:8,** What 8 things are we to think about?

_____
_____
_____

4. Keep your mind stayed on God.

In **Isaiah 26:3,** this is a promise for all people of all ages who meet the condition of keeping their mind stayed on God and who always trust in Him in all things and in all places. What does this create in us when we do these things?

_____

_____

5. Use the weapons of spiritual warfare.

In reading **2 Corinthians 10:4-6**, what are the weapons of our warfare, and what do they pull down?

_____

_____

_____

What is cast down?

_____

_____

What punishes all disobedience when we use this weapon of our warfare?

_____

_____

6. Put on the whole armor of God.

In **Ephesians 6:10-18**, Why do we put on the whole armor of God?

_____
_____

What do we wrestle against?

_____
_____
_____

In **v 13,** What ability will be given us when we put on the whole armor of God?

_____
_____

In **v 14,** What do we put on our waist; what is the breastplate for?

_____
_____

In **v 15,** Explain what is on the feet and what this prepares you

God's WORD Sets You Free

for.
_____
_____

It is important to understand that **verse 15** speaks of preparedness; readiness. It is the gospel of making peace with God and of readiness to meet Him.

In **verses 15-17,** what other parts of the armor are we to take? How important is prayer in preparing for the enemy?
_____
_____
_____
_____

7. Have faith in God.

In **Matthew 6:25-34** Jesus addresses the importance of worrying. Read these verses and explain the importance of getting to know God in a real way in order to leave things to Him. What should we seek first? What can "worry" not do for you?
_____
_____
_____

8. Live and walk in the Spirit.

Galatians 5:16-26, Describe the works of the flesh and the fruit of the Spirit.

_____
_____
_____
_____

9. Do not cast away confidence.

In **Hebrew 3:14**, What do we become if we hold onto our confidence?

_____
_____

After warning the Christians that they can fall into sin and apostasy and be cut off from God by sin as Israel was, the apostle lays down the condition they must meet to be finally saved.

It is to hold the original confidence steadfast until the end. We all struggle with confidence, but when losing, it causes us to stray away, going away from God completely; they are being warned about this.

10. Cast all care upon God.

In **1 Peter 5:7,** what does it say about God?

_____

_____

Meditate On

What we put into our minds determines what comes out in our words and actions. Paul tells us to program our minds with thoughts that are true, honorable, right, pure, lovely, admirable, excellent, and worthy of praise.

It's important to look at the things that we engage in on a regular basis so that we keep ourselves going in the right direction. Above all things, we need to implement time for reading God's Word into our daily schedule and praying. Like anything, it takes practice.

In **Philippians 4:8,** we read:

> "Finally, brethren, whatever things are true, whatever things are noble, whatever things are just, whatever things are pure, whatever things are lovely, whatever things are of good report, if there is any virtue and if there is anything praiseworthy – meditate on these things." (Philippians 4:8; NKJV)

When we understand that the words that come out of our mouth plant seeds, we realized the importance of not planting bad seeds. What you sow, you reap. What comes out of your mouth is a result of your thoughts, your understanding, and your attitude. Meditating is thinking in alignment with what you currently understand to be true and necessary, often what benefits you. But what benefits us may not be what is good to bring forth.

God wants all to experience His love, care, and provision. This is why we must consider what we meditate on and how it will affect not only us but those around us. This is how God cares for us. He always considers the end result in all things

In **Isaiah 55**, God reveals that His declared word becomes creative. Just as God created with "words," saying "be," and it was, we are to do the same with our words. But if we don't think about the right things, we won't create what's of God. Our words need to be in alignment with God's Word when we declare it in faith. This is a *creative seed* that will grow and produce after its kind.

The Word endues us with power for all good works **(2 Timothy 3:16-17)**.

In **v 17,** what is the end result God wants for us, and what does it equip us with?

_____

_____

6 Things to Meditate On (Philippians 4:8)

1. **True things**; all that is in harmony with eternal truth in creation and revelation. **(2 Timothy 2:15; 3:16-17)**.

2. **Noble things**; all that is pure, reverent, honorable, and Christian. The Greek word used here is *semnos*. **(1 Timothy 3:8, 11; Titus 2:2)**.

3. **Just things**; all that is in harmony with justice and righteousness. **(Romans 3:24-31; 8:4; 2 Peter 1:4-10)**.

4. **Pure things**; all that is chaste and holy for body and

soul. **(Romans 12:1-2; 1 Corinthians 3:16-17; 2 Corinthians 7:1).**

5. **Lovely things**; all that is pleasing and tends to bless others. **(1 Corinthians 13:4-8; Galatians 5:22-23).**

6. **Things of good report**; all that is in harmony with the best public good; virtuous and praiseworthy. **(Romans 13:1-10; 2 Peter 1:4-10).**

What is your hardest struggle in your thinking, and how can you begin to change and become more like God desires?

_____
_____

Faith Builder

Faith must be more than belief in certain facts; it must result in action, growth in Christian character, and the practice of moral discipline, or it will die away **(James 2:14-17).**

Our faith must go beyond what we believe; it must become a dynamic part of all we do, resulting in good fruit and spiritual maturity.

Salvation does not depend on good deeds but results in good

deeds. A person who claims to be saved while remaining unchanged does not understand faith or what God has done for them.

Peter lists several of faith's actions: learning to know God better, developing perseverance, doing God's will, and loving others. These actions do not come automatically but require hard work. They are not optional; they must be a continual part of the Christian life. We don't finish one and start on the next, but we work on them all together. God empowers and enables us, but He also gives us the responsibility to learn and grow.

False teachers said self-control was unnecessary because deeds do not help the believer anyway **(2 Peter 1:6; 2:19)**. It is true that deeds cannot save us, but it is false to think they are unimportant. We are saved so that we can grow to resemble Christ and serve others. God wants to produce His character in us. But to do this, He encourages our discipline and effort. As we obey Christ, who guides us by His Spirit, we will develop self-control not only with respect to food and drink but also with respect to emotions and actions.

In **2 Peter 2:19 (NLT)**, what are we a slave to?

_____

7 Steps In Spiritual Arithmetic (2 Peter 1:5-7)

1. But also for this very reason, giving all diligence, add to your faith _____. (v 5)
2. Add to virtue _____. (v 5)
3. Add to knowledge _____. (v 6)
4. Add to self-control _____. (v 6)
5. Add to perseverance _____. (v 6)
6. Add to godliness _____. (v 7)
7. Add to brotherly kindness _____. (v 7).

As we close out this study, it is good to know the background of **1 and 2 Peter.**

1 Peter was written just before the Roman emperor Nero began his persecution of Christians. **2 Peter** was written two or three years later (between A.D. 66 and 68) after persecution had intensified. **1 Peter** was a letter of encouragement to the Christians who suffered, but **2 Peter** focuses on the church's internal problems, especially the false teachers causing people to doubt their faith and turn away from Christianity. **2 Peter** combats their heresies by denouncing the evil motives of the false teachers and reaffirming Christianity's truths, the authority of Scripture, the primacy of faith, and the certainty of Christ's return.

God's WORD Sets You Free

Many believers want an abundance of God's grace and peace, but they are unwilling to put forth the effort to get to know Him better through Bible study and prayer. To enjoy God's privileges freely, we must grow in our knowledge of God and Jesus, our Lord and Savior, and the Holy Spirit.

The power to lead a godly life comes from God. Because we don't have the resources to be truly godly, God allows us to *"share His divine nature"* in order to keep us from sin and help us live for Him.

When we are born again, God, by His Spirit, empowers us with His own goodness. **(John 3:6; 14:17-23; 2 Corinthians 5:21; and 1 Peter 1:22, 23).**

In **John 14:17,** what does it say as the reason why the world cannot receive the Spirit of Truth?

___

What do you think is the solution to be able to receive the Spirit of Truth?

___

In **John 14:18,** what does it say that God will not leave us as?

___

In **John 14:21,** what does Jesus promise us and how do we know we will receive it?

_____
_____

In **1 Peter 1:22-25,** what gives us the power and endures forever?

_____

Power of One Voice, LLC
Come Alive Series

13

The Goodness of God

> "Look at the birds of the air, for they neither sow nor reap nor gather into barns; yet your heavenly Father feeds them. Are you not of more value than they?" (Matthew 6:26; NKJV)

To see the goodness of our Heavenly Father, we must first be willing to put away the "worry" we commonly carry in our walk of life.

In **Matthew 6:25-34** Jesus spoke clearly to not worry. It is part of His explanation of "double-mindedness."

Double-mindedness is a product of fear, doubt, and ignorance. We think about many things, but we allow wrong things to take the power away from the good thoughts God has meant for us.

Spiritual vision is our capacity to see clearly what God wants us to do and to see the world from His point of view. But this spiritual insight can be easily clouded. Self-serving desires, interests, and goals block that vision. Serving God is the best way to restore it.

One way to correct our vision is through the eye. How we see things not only through physical manifestation but also through our understanding; can only be improved upon and fully transformed by reading God's Word.

A "good" eye is one that is fixed on God.

For instance, the explanation in **Matthew 6:22-23** reads;

> "The lamp of the body is the eye. If therefore, your eye is good, your whole body will be full of light. But if your eye is bad, your whole body will be full of darkness. If therefore the light that is in you is darkness, how great is that darkness?" (Matthew 6:22-23; NKJV)

When we read God's Word, we think about the right things, but when we venture back into the world, we think about things of the world. Therefore, your alone time with God must be consistent and daily.

In **Matthew 6:25-34** Jesus teaches about worry, and we see eight *reasons why we should not worry*. Let's look at God's desire for our ability to thrive in the life He has given us by addressing these eight reasons why we *shouldn't* worry.

Because of the ill effects of worry, Jesus tells us not to worry about the needs God promises to supply. Worry may damage your health, disrupt your ability to live life, negatively affect the way you treat others, and reduce your ability to trust in God. The difference between worry and genuine concern is that *worry immobilizes*, but concern moves you to action.

To seek the Kingdom of God above all else means to put God first in your life, to fill your thoughts with His desires, to take His character for your pattern, and to serve and obey Him in everything. Planning for tomorrow is time well spent. Worrying about tomorrow is time wasted. Sometimes it's difficult to tell the difference.

Careful planning is thinking ahead about goals, steps, and schedules and trusting in God's guidance. When done well, planning can help alleviate worry. Worriers, by contrast, are consumed by fear and find it difficult to trust God. They let their plans interfere with their relationship with God. Don't let worries about tomorrow affect your relationship with God today.

8 Reasons Why We Should Not Worry

1. **Life is more than food (v 25).**
2. **The body is more than clothing.**
3. **Men are greater than materials.**
4. **Men are greater than birds that God feeds without their labor (v 26).**
5. **Worry cannot change the body (v 27).**
6. **Men are better than plants that do not worry about clothing (v 28-30).**
7. **God's providence is over all creation, not only birds and plants that never buy, sell, manufacture, or labor (v 26-32).**
8. **Worry is useless and sinful and must not be tolerated (v 33-34).**

When you know and understand God's desire for all His creation, you see those things such as "worry" only take you down a long, *useless* road that never causes you to draw closer to Him.

If you want the power to live your life as God intended, it is of utmost importance to put away things that *don't serve you*. Worry is only one thing that hijacks us from serving God in faith.

Have you thought of what "worrying" might produce or hinder you in?

Worrying Ruins God's Plan In Our Lives in these ways:

1. **Sinful; and produces fear.**
2. **A disease-causing other ill.**
3. **Borrowing trouble that cannot be paid back.**
4. **Brooding over what may not happen.**
5. **Creating trouble, misery, and death.**
6. **A burden borrowed from tomorrow and from others who should carry it.**
7. **A weight that kills prematurely.**
8. **Mental and physical suicide.**
9. **A grave digger that has no sympathy.**
10. **Needless and wastes time and effort that should be spent on worthwhile things.**
11. **A robber of faith, peace, and trust in a never-failing, heavenly Father.**
12. **A stumbling block for others.**
13. **A disgrace to God that should never be indulged in by Christians.**
14. **Anxiety over what is nothing today and less tomorrow, in view of faith.**

15. **Anticipating troubles that seldom come to those who trust God.**
16. **Torment over something that will likely be a blessing if it comes.**
17. **Living like an orphan without a heavenly Father.**
18. **A crime against God, man, nature, and better judgment.**
19. **Mental cruelty to self and others.**
20. **Foolish, for whatever is going to happen cannot be stopped by worry; and if it doesn't happen, there is nothing to worry about—should adversity come, one may still be victorious by trusting in God.**

This thing of worrying is something most of us encounter in life. It's how we react to experiences in life. But we must get off the path blinding us to see God's goodness.

We see this in a story in **Luke 10** of Martha, the older sister of Mary and Lazarus, and how she was so absorbed in "doing" that she couldn't be in the present moment, appreciating the visitation of Jesus.

The fact is that Martha, Mary, and Lazarus are all remembered for their hospitality. We see into their world with an added significance of why this was important in their day, a social requirement in their culture.

In **Luke 10:38-42** we see the story. Martha was a worrier. She worried about the details. She wanted to please, serve, and do the right thing—but she often made everyone around her uncomfortable.

Martha's frustration was so intense that Jesus had to speak up. He gently corrected her attitude and showed her that her priorities, though good, were not the best in this situation.

What we see in Jesus and how he *gently* helps us understand by correcting us is exactly how God is. Jesus said when you see me, you see the Father.

There are many things we can learn and improve from, but there is something so sure, so real that stands as our foundation, that will never change, and that is God's Providence.

In providence, God assumes responsibility for the eternal care of the universe. Providence means foresight and forethought, the care of God over His creatures, and the divine office over *all things*.

God didn't just create us and place us in the world He created to live in, but He created us to thrive, to become more, and to create. God did this because He longs for us to be an extension of Himself.

We are not here to just submit and crawl into a little corner, waiting for Him to take us home in death. We have a future;

here, we learn how to withstand the enemy and thrive in following God in everything.

Foresight and forethought on the part of anybody imply a future end, a goal, and a definite plan for attaining that end. In other words, God has a plan for each of us, and it is wonderful.

God doesn't do everything randomly or half-heartedly. God doesn't just accept the evil in this world as taking over but is still waiting, longing for each to turn back to Him after they see that their path is only hurting themselves.

God is Love; love suffers long and is kind; love does not envy; love does not parade itself, is not puffed up; does not behave rudely, does not seek its own, is not provoked, thinks no evil; does not rejoice in iniquity, but rejoices in the truth; bears all things, believes all things, hopes all things, and endures all things. Love never fails.

If you want to know Our Father in His pure state, remember that God is all the above things in "love" and more. It has become very clear to me that we don't know God, Our Heavenly Father, and it is tragic, to say the least.

If we knew Him as He is, we would never do what we do. Religious acts say they love you but don't love you if you don't belong to their church. Most of us don't know the love that created us, but it's time we *begin* to see it, and this is why we must study the Word of God.

Providence of God

Although all rational beings exercise providence according to their powers, the word "providence" reaches its full significance only when it is applied to the infinite God.

The providence of God is the care, preservation, and government He exercises over *all things* He has created in order that they may accomplish the ends for which they were created.

It is the infinite care God takes of His universe, from the numbering of each hair on each head and the falling of each sparrow to the unfailing upholding of all the vast universes by His own power. That eternal power is at work, excluding all fortune, luck, and chance.

God promises to meet the needs of man. All the promises of God reveal that He has provided for man here and now despite the curse from Satan.

Everyone can enjoy to the fullest all the benefits of these promises if he will surrender his life to God, experience the genuine New Birth, and live a godly life in this present world according to the gospel of Christ.

And even more important is that God extends these benefits

even to the unsaved to prove to them that God provides for all creation despite their rebellion.

The purpose of such goodness to the unsaved is to lead to repentance, as we read in **Romans 2:4**;

> "Or do you despise the riches of His goodness, forbearance, and longsuffering, not knowing that the goodness of God leads you to repentance?" (Romans 2:4; NKJV)

When Paul's letter **(Romans 2)** was read in the Roman church, no doubt many heads nodded as he condemned idol worshipers, homosexual practices, and violent people. But what surprise his listeners must have felt when he turned on them and said in effect, "You are just as bad, and you have no excuse!" Paul was emphatically stressing that we have all sinned repeatedly, and there is no way apart from Christ to be saved from sin's consequences.

However, in Romans, Paul continues to share the way of salvation.

1. **Everyone has sinned. (Romans 3:23)**
2. **The penalty for our sins is death. (Romans 6:23)**
3. **Jesus Christ died for sin. (Romans 5:8)**

4. To be forgiven for our sins, we must believe and confess that Jesus is Lord. Salvation comes through Jesus Christ. (Romans 10:8-10)

The longsuffering is the leniency and patience of God whereby God's mercy and goodness are extended to men to bring them to eternal reconciliation with Himself.

God holds back His judgment in His kindness, giving people time to turn from their sins. It is easy to mistake God's patience for approval of the wrong way we are living.

Self-evaluation is difficult, and it is even more difficult to bring ourselves to God and let Him tell us where we need to change. But as Christians, we must ask God to point out our sins so that He can heal them.

Unfortunately, we are more likely to be amazed at God's patience with others than humbled at His patience with us.

And in **2 Peter 3:9,** we read;

> **"The Lord is not slack concerning His promise, as some count slackness, but is longsuffering toward us, not willing that any should perish but that all should come to repentance." (2 Peter 3:9; NKJV)**

This shows us why God has delayed so long in putting down all rebellion and tolerating His enemies to continue their evil designs.

God wants the *best opportunity* for us, and He is always trying to get us to stop doing evil and start living with Him.

All through Scripture, we read of God's mercy and desire for each of us no matter what we have done in the past.

Let us look where scripture teaches that it is God's will for man to be blessed.

God wants **prosperity** for us all, but the only path that can bring us what will heal us and help us feel whole; is simply being obedient to God's commands.

In my walk with God, I have become very aware that God only wants the best for us, and we cannot experience it when walking against our *best interests* when living for ourselves and ignoring God.

We are created by God, and He has so much waiting to give us, so much for us to embrace, but we can't begin if we don't begin to remove everything that will hurt us.

For example, if you are holding onto anger from the past, it's like a hot coal in your hand. You will continue to get burnt for as long as *you choose* to do this.

The only way to experience the greater joy of overcoming is to put down that hot coal and walk away.

God wants you to take your own free will and choose that you will no longer take that path; of holding onto the past. God wants you to make your own choice and begin again.

The past is over, and you couldn't do anything about it if you wanted to. God forgives you instantly, completely wiping clean your past, so why don't you do that for others?

God's goodness to all of us is to give us a new opportunity to begin again. Can you do that for others?

In **Joshua 1:5** we read;

> **"No man shall be able to stand before you all the days of your life; as I was with Moses, so I will be with you. I will not leave you nor forsake you." (Joshua 1:5; NKJV)**

Here again, we read that God never leaves us alone. God stays with us, but the further we get from God, the more alone *we feel*. It is our *"belief"* that God left us, that lies to us daily, telling us we have no one who cares. Satan reinforces this so we will become trapped in our own "beliefs."

Here we read in Joshua 1:5 of Joshua's new job. It consisted of leading more than two million people into a strange new land and conquering it. Without God leading and guiding him, it could have been frightening. With God by his side, it could then be an adventure.

Just as God was with Joshua, He is with us as we encounter new challenges. We may not conquer nations, but we face tough situations, difficult people, and temptations every day. However, God promises that He will never abandon or fail to help us. By asking God to direct us, we can conquer many of life's challenges.

God has laid the foundations of the earth and set the earth upon them, and by virtue of creation, He is the owner of all things. God has created every opportunity for us to begin again.

In **1 Samuel 2:7-8** we read;

> "The LORD makes poor and makes rich; He brings low and lifts up. He raises the poor from the dust and lifts the beggar from the ash heap, to set them among princes and make them inherit the throne of glory. For

> the pillars of the earth are the LORD's, and He has set the world upon them." (1 Samuel 2:7-8; NKJV)

Material prosperity is as much the will of God as soul and body health. See also in **Deuteronomy 8:18; Job 1:21; 5:10-11; 36:7; 38:4-7; 42:10; Psalm 75:7; James 2:5).**

In **Deuteronomy 8:18**, we read:

> "Remember the LORD your God. He is the one who gives you power to be successful, in order to fulfill the covenant He confirmed to your ancestors with an oath." (Deuteronomy 8:18; NLT)

In times of plenty, we often take credit for our prosperity and become proud that our own hard work and cleverness have made us rich. It is easy to get so busy collecting and managing wealth that we push God right out of our lives. But it is God who gives us everything we have, and it is God who asks us to manage it for Him.

In **Job 36:11,** we read:

> "If they listen and obey God, they will be blessed with prosperity throughout their lives. All their years will be pleasant." (Job 36:11; NLT)

In **Job 42:10,** we read:

> "When Job prayed for his friends, the LORD restored his fortunes. In fact, the LORD gave him twice as much as before!" (Job 42:10; NLT)

After receiving so much criticism, Job was still able to pray for his three friends. It is difficult to forgive someone who has accused us of wrongdoing, but Job did.

Would the message of the Book of Job change if God had not restored to Job his former blessings? No. God is still sovereign. Jesus said anyone who gives up something for the Kingdom of God will be repaid **(Luke 18:29-30)**.

Our restoration may or may not be the same kind as Job's, which was both spiritual and material. Our complete restoration may not be in this life - but it will happen. God loves us, and He is always just. Cling tightly to your faith through all your trials, and you, too, will be rewarded by God -- if not now, in the life to come.

In **Psalms 1:1-3** we read;

> "Blessed is the man who walks not in the counsel of the ungodly, nor stands in the path of sinners, nor sits in the seat of the scornful; But his delight is in the law of the LORD, And in His law he meditates day and night. He shall be like a tree planted by the rivers of water, that brings forth its fruit in its season, Whose leaf also shall not wither; And whatever he does shall prosper." (Psalms 1:1-3; NKJV)

In **3 John 2**, we read;

> "Beloved, I pray that you may prosper in all things and in health, just as your soul prospers." (3 John 2; NKJV)

If such blessings are the will of God for one person, then they are His will for all men who will have faith in them because there is no partiality in the gospel.

It is also God's will for man to be blessed with **healing**

and health. Christ came to destroy the works of the devil **(1 John 3:8)** and to deliver "all that were oppressed by the devil" **(Acts 10:38).**

He came to do this not only for 3 years during His ministry but forever.

Christ commissioned the disciples to carry on the work He began to do and teach. Early believers did carry on this work until they lost faith.

In **Matthew 8:17**, we read;

> "That it might be fulfilled which was spoken by Isaiah the prophet, saying: 'He Himself took our infirmities and bore our sicknesses.'" (Matthew 8:17; NKJV)

No man can expect to be immune from sickness unless he meets the conditions, but every man can expect such blessings when he meets them.

In **Exodus 15:26**, we read;

> "And said, 'If you diligently heed the voice of the

> LORD your God and do what is right in His sight, give ear to His commandments and keep all His statutes, I will put none of the diseases on you which I have brought on the Egyptians. For I am the LORD who heals you." (Exodus 15:26; NKJV)

And in **Psalms 91**, we read;

> "He who dwells in the secret place of the Most High shall abide under the shadow of the Almighty.....Surely He shall deliver you...from the perilous pestilence....A thousand shall fall at your side, and ten thousand at your right hand, but it shall not come near you...No evil shall befall you, nor shall any plague come near your dwelling." (Psalms 91; NKJV)

The scriptures prove that Divine providence has been working in all ages in all the affairs of men.

It was providence that originally brought all things into existence **(Isaiah 45:18; Colossians 1:15-19)**, that provided redemption for the fall **(Genesis 3:15; Ephesians 1:1-11)** that preserved the race at the flood **(Genesis 6:8-8:22)**, and that dealt with men in each dispensation giving them a chance to make good in every age.

The continued preservation of all things from the creation of man proves that God's providence is working out all things after the counsel of ***His own will.***

God's purpose has been to create a race of beings who would find their highest degree of happiness in the highest degree of holiness and who would glorify their creator in proportion to their highest holiness and happiness. **(Genesis 1:26-28; Isaiah 43:7; 45:18; Ephesians 1:12; Colossians 1:15-22; Revelations 4:9-11; 5:11-14; 7:10-12).**

In **Psalms 8,** we see that God's name is excellent in all the earth, and His glory is higher than the heavens.

He has been greatly magnified by the gospel in this age of grace.

Psalms 8:4 we read;

> **"What is man that You are mindful of him, And the son of man that You visit him?" (Psalms 8:1-4; NKJV)**

The Hebrew word for "mindful" is *zakar which means to mark or remember* **continually,** *as perpetual incense rising; to set the heart upon; to keep* **continually** *in merciful view.*

God is mindful of man, and we are always on His mind. The Hebrew word *zakar*, translated as mindful, is found over 170 times. **(Psalms 8:4; 111:5; 115:12; Nehemiah 9:17; Isaiah 17:10 are a few).**

That God should remember in mercy such miserable beings is great condescension; that He should visit them by assuming their own nature, dwelling among them, and giving His life a ransom for them, **is mercy and love indescribable and divine.**

7 Ways God Visits Man (Psalms 8:4)

1. **By coming Himself (Daniel 7:9-14).**
2. **By sending Christ (Isaiah 48:16; John 3:16).**
3. **By sending the Holy Spirit (John 16:7).**
4. **By sending Angels (Hebrew 1:14).**
5. **By Prophets (Acts 3:21; Hebrews 1:1).**
6. **By dreams and visions (Daniel 2:28; 4:1-7; 7:1; 8:1; etc.).**
7. **By His Word (2 Timothy 3:16; Hebrews 4:12).**

4 General Acts of Providence
Psalms 111:5-6

1. **God provides food (v 5).**
2. **He constantly seeks to carry out His covenant responsibility.**
3. **He manifests His great power and works with His people (v 6).**
4. **He plans that His people inherit the earth and its fullness (v 6; Psalms 37:9, 29; Matthew 5:5).**

It is a wonderful thing that God provides food, He constantly seeks to carry out His covenant responsibility, He manifests His great power and works to help His people, and He plans that His people shall inherit the earth and its fullness. **(Psalms 37:9; Matthew 5:5)**

In **Nehemiah 9:17,** we see how God continued to be patient with His people. In spite of our repeated failings, pride, and stubbornness, God is always ready to forgive.

> "They refused to obey, and they were not mindful of Your wonders that You did among them. But they hardened their necks, and in their rebellion they appointed a leader to return to their bondage. But You

> are God, ready to pardon, gracious and merciful, slow to anger, abundant in kindness, and did not forsake them." (Nehemiah 9:17; NKJV)

This verse refers to **Exodus 32**, where the people said of the golden calf that it was the god who had led them out of Egypt. After all that God did, they refused to give Him credit, yet God stayed with them.

In **Isaiah 16:10-11** we read that they had forgotten God, neglected salvation, and had not been mindful that true help and protection come from God. God and Christ were the great Rocks of Israel. When they set out plants and hope for a good crop, they would be disappointed because of the invader taking it. They would have grief and sorrow.

Numbers 14:4, they said they would elect a leader to take them back to Egypt.

In **Exodus 33:18-19** we see a new revelation revealed to Moses of God.

> "And he said, "Please, show me Your glory." Then He said, "I will make all My goodness pass before you, and I will proclaim the name of the LORD before you. I will

> be gracious to whom I will be gracious, and I will have compassion on whom I will have compassion." (Exodus 33:18-19; NKJV)

Moses asked to see God's glory as expressed in His face or countenance, not to see His face apart from His glory.

That he had seen God's literal face is clearly stated in **v 11**, and that he had seen God's glory in a limited sense is clear from **Exodus 16:10; 24:16-17**. This request was for something he had not yet seen.

Beyond showing Moses His glory as expressed in His back or the after-effects and glimpse of the glory after it had passed by, as is stated in **Exodus 33:20-23**, God gave Moses a greater revelation of His character and infinite nature.

The Hebrew word for *goodness* in **Exodus 33:19** is *tuwb*, which means supreme, outstanding quality, expressing the highest quality of goodness.

The word *"proclaim"* in that same verse simply means that God would announce to Moses (while hidden in the cleft of the rock) who He was as He passed by so that Moses would know it was Jehovah and not an angel whose back he saw after the hand was removed as written about in **v 22**. In **v 22,** this affirms that it was God in His infinite glory that Moses wanted to see in his request in **v 18** and God's answer in **v 22**.

In the statement in **v 19**, *"I will be gracious to whom I will be gracious, and I will have compassion on whom I will have compassion,";* it is here that God makes it clear that no act of grace or mercy was merited by man, but that His own will was the basis of all His blessings.

In other words, they do not come from God simply because man wills it to be, but because God is essentially good, gracious, merciful and does everything for man after His own free choice, it is *His pleasure to will that man be blessed* (**v 19; Exodus 34:5-7; Romans 9:15; Ephesians 1:5, 11; Revelations 4:11**).

In **Exodus 34:5,** Moses ascended, and the Lord descended to meet him on the mount. Here God stood by Moses again, face to face as before.

If it had been an invisible presence, Moses could not have written such simple facts which indicate he *saw* the Lord standing there.

> "Now the LORD descended in the cloud and stood with him there, and proclaimed the name of the LORD."
> (Exodus 34:5; NKJV)

The Hebrew word *qara* is used for "proclaimed" and means to approach a person met; call out to; address by name; introduce or announce self; publish; pronounce; or make a proclamation.

There are 10 Names and Attributes of God proclaimed by Himself.

1. **Hebrew *Jehovah***
2. **Hebrew *El Jehovah*, Strong Jehovah.**
3. **Hebrew *rachuwm*, merciful, full of tenderness and compassion.**
4. **Hebrew *channuwn*, gracious.**
5. **Hebrew *arek aph*, long-suffering, not easily angered or irritated.**
6. **Hebrew *rab checed*, abundant and sufficient in goodness, kindness, and love.**
7. **Hebrew *emeth*, truth, trustworthiness, and faithfulness.**
8. **Hebrew *natsar checed*, guarding or protecting, kindness and mercy.**
9. **Hebrew *nasa avon pesha chattaah*, lifting up and carrying away moral evil, perversity, moral and religious revolt, and all offenses.**

10. **Hebrew *paqad avon*, overseeing punishment for moral evil.**

These things combine to give the real meaning of the word *"Jehovah."* Thus, He is all things to all men. God exercises all the above qualities in His many dealings with men—manifesting strength, mercy, tenderness, compassion, graciousness, longsuffering, goodness, kindness, love, faithfulness, trustworthiness, and moral cleansing, as well as administering punishments whenever they are needed.

In **Luke 6:35-36** we see where Jesus speaks on the laws of mercy.

> "But love your enemies, do good, and lend, hoping for nothing in return; and your reward will be great, and you will be sons of the Most High. For He is kind to the unthankful and evil. Therefore be merciful, just as your Father also is merciful." (Luke 6:35-36; NKJV)

In **verse 35,** the Greek word for "kind," referring to God being kind, is *chrestos,* and it means morally good, kind, and generous. It is one of the fruits of the Spirit, as we read in **Galatians 5:21-22.**

Commands to be good are found in: **(Leviticus 19:34; Luke 6:35-36; Romans 15:1-5; Galatians 6:10; Ephesians 4:32; Colossians 3:12-14; 1 Peter 3:8; 4:8; 2 Peter 1:7; 1 John 3:17-18).**

God has never hidden from us.

Adam and Eve saw God in visible form after they had sinned and hid from Him "among the trees of the garden" because "they heard the sound of the Lord God walking in the garden" **(Genesis 3:8-19).** They could not hide behind a tree from God in His invisible presence, which is everywhere.

Cain saw God in visible form, for he could not have been driven out of the invisible presence which is with everyone everywhere **(Genesis 4:6, 9, 16)**

It is clear from **Genesis 11:5** that God appeared on earth at the time of the tower of Babel, for it says, "The Lord came down to see the city and the tower."

God appeared to Isaac and confirmed the Abrahamic covenant with him, as Genesis 26:2-4 clearly states, "the Lord appeared to him."

There is a total of **44 appearances of God to man**, and they include these already mentioned as well as others. Others include Jacob, Moses, Aaron, Miriam, Balaam, a donkey, Joshua,

Israel, Gideon, Manoah's wife, Samuel, Elijah, David, Job, Ezekiel, Daniel, Isaiah, Zechariah, Amos, Stephen, and John.

In view of the above appearances of God to men, the often-quoted verse, "No one has seen God at any time" **(John 1:18)**, can only be understood to mean that no man has seen Him face to face in His glory and comprehended Him fully as "the only begotten Son, who is in the bosom of the Father," who "has declared Him.

God dwells in infinite glory, which no man has ever seen nor can see. God, out of His glory, has been seen many times with the eyes of men.

Moses talked with God face to face out of His glory, and when he said, "Please show me Your glory," his request could not be granted except as manifested through a glimpse of God's back **(Exodus 33:11-23).**

14

"The Goodness of God" Study

Further Study

The Doctrine of Providence

Providence means foresight and forethought, all from God. His care over His creatures, divine superintendence over all things. Knowing that foresight and forethought on the part of anybody implies a future end, a goal, and a definite plan for attaining that end. In providence, God assumes responsibility for the eternal care of the universe. It takes in the provision for and preservation of His creation in all eternity.

Promises for the Needs of Man

All the promises of God reveal that He has provided for man here and now despite the curse. Everyone can fully enjoy all the benefits of these promises if he surrenders his life to God, experience the genuine New Birth, and lives a godly life in this present world according to the gospel of Christ. Many of these benefits are even for the unsaved to prove God provides for all creation despite their rebellion. The purpose of such goodness to the unsaved is to lead to repentance. **(Romans 2:4).**

What three things lead to repentance, as stated in **Romans 2:4?**

1. _____

2. _____

3. _____

God's Will For Man to Be Blessed

1. *Prosperity* **(Joshua 1:5-9; 1 Samuel 2:7-8; 1 Kings 2:3-4; 1 Chronicles 29:12; Ezra 8:22; Job 36:11; Psalm 1:1-3; Matthew 6:31-33; 7:7-11; Mark 11:22-24; John 15:7, 16; 2 Corinthians 9:6-8; Philippians 4:19; 1 Timothy 6:17-19; 3 John 2).** God

God's WORD Sets You Free

wants us to have more than enough. Poverty is a lie from the enemy to keep us in bondage.

In **1 Timothy 6:17-19** does God say He gives us the riches?

_____

Are the riches to be condemned or enjoyed **(v 17)**?

_____

In **3 John 2**, what is God's will for all saints? (also see **Psalm 1:3)**?

_____

In **Joshua 1:8,** what is the secret of success?

_____

2. *Healing and Health* **(Exodus 15:26; Psalm 91; 103:3-5; Isaiah 53:4-5; 58:8; Matthew 8:16-17; James 5:14-16; 1 Peter 2:24; 3 John 2).** Christ came to "destroy the works of the devil" **(1 John 3:8)** and to deliver "all that were oppressed by the devil" **(Acts 10:38).**

In **1 John 3:8,** the Son of God was manifested that He might destroy what?

___

Where did Jesus go after His death? What did He bring home to heaven when He returned? **(Ephesians 4:8-10; Psalms 68:18; Hebrews 2:14-15)**

___

He came to do this (healing) not only for 3 years during His ministry but forever. He commissioned the disciples to carry on the work He began to do and teach **(Matthew 28:19-20; Mark 16:15-20; John 14:12-15; Acts 1:1-2, 8).** Early believers did carry on this work until they lost faith **(Acts 3; 5:16; James 5:14-16, etc.)**

Present Christians are to contend for the faith once delivered to the saints **(Jude 3; 2 Corinthians 10:4-6; Ephesians 6:10-18).**

3. *Wants and needs.* (Psalm 23:1-6; 34:9-10; 37:3-6; 84:11; Mark 9:23; 11:22-24; John 14:12-15; 15:7, 16; 16:23-26; 1 John 3:21-22; 5:14-15).

Name 4 things that the LORD is to His people.
(Psalm 23)

1. _____
2. _____
3. _____
4. _____

The All-Bountiful Promises of God

1. *Salvation* (Psalm 50:23; Romans 10:9-10; 1:16; Acts 2:21; 4:12; 2 Thessalonians 2:13; Titus 2:11-14; Hebrews 7:25).

2. *Prosperity* (1 Samuel 2:7-8; 1 Kings 2:3-4; 1 Chronicles 29:12; Ezra 8:22; Job 36:11; Psalm 1:1-3; 3 John 2; Matthew 7:7-11; 17:20; 21:22; Mark 11:22-24; John 14:12-15; 15:7, 16; 16:23-26; 2 Corinthians 9:6-8).

3. *Healing and Health* (Exodus 15:26; Psalm 91; 103:3-5; Isaiah 53:3-5; 58:8; Matthew 8:16-17; Mark 16:15-20; James 5:14-16; 1 Peter 2:24; 3 John 2).

4. *All wants and needs* (Psalm 23:1; Psalm 34:9-10; Psalm 84:11; Matthew 17:20; Matthew 21:22; Mark 9:23; Mark 11:22-24; John 14: 12-15; John 15:7; John 15:16; John

16:23-26; James 1:4-8; 1 John 3:21-22; 5:13-14; Hebrews 11:6).

Ultimate Purpose of Providence

God's purpose has been to create a race of beings who would find their highest degree of happiness in the highest degree of holiness and who would glorify their Creator in proportion to their highest holiness and happiness. **(Genesis 1:26-28; Isaiah 43:7; 45:18; Ephesians 1:12; Colossians 1:15-22; Revelations 4:9-11; 5:11-14; 7:10-12).**

When you understand that God is giving free-will choices to all of us and His hope is that we will rule and reign with Him, does this give you a new perspective on the nature of our Heavenly Father?

_____

To fully embark on all that you can do, you must be in alignment with the same things that created you. This is why doing the right things, living according to the WORD, and staying away from all that hinders you; are actually in your best interest.

God's WORD Sets You Free

What are your feelings now when you understand things from the perspective that God wants you to rule and reign with Him by your side?

_____
_____
_____
_____
_____

Note on all the answers in the study guide:

Many of these answers are to search out scripture because our Father wants you to do that. He wants you to engage in the search and to let Him speak to you, answers that can help you grow in understanding. We have an amazing Heavenly Father...let us all begin a journey to get to know His heart that is so full of love for all His creation. Anything not like His true nature is of the enemy, and Satan doesn't want you to know Him. Satan has lied, slandered, and cast all the evil that Satan has done himself upon God. Take a fresh new look and discover a Father that is so precious, so mysteriously in love with all creation, and only wants the best for all of us. God wants His children to come home so He can spoil, love, and engage with us in ruling, reigning, and creating more for all eternity.

Power of One Voice, LLC
Come Alive Series

www.ingramcontent.com/pod-product-compliance
Lightning Source LLC
Chambersburg PA
CBHW071226080526
44587CB00013BA/1508